Being
Mystic

In Touch With God

Betsy Balega

BOOKS

Winchester, UK
Washington, USA

First published by O-Books, 2011
O-Books is an imprint of John Hunt Publishing Ltd., Laurel House, Station Approach,
Alresford, Hants, SO24 9JH, UK
office1@o-books.net
www.o-books.com

For distributor details and how to order please visit the 'Ordering' section on our website.

ISBN: 978 1 84694 528 1

A CIP catalogue record for this book is available from the British Library.

Design: Stuart Davies

Printed in the UK by CPI Antony Rowe
Printed in the USA by Offset Paperback Mfrs, Inc

We operate a distinctive and ethical publishing philosophy in all
areas of our business, from our global network of authors to
production and worldwide distribution.

CONTENTS

Being
Mystic

In Touch With God

In Being Mystic: In Touch With God, *Betsy Balega describes the development of her psychic abilities and how she incorporated the gift of "second sight" into her daily life. The book also provides helpful suggestions on how we can contact our own spirit guides and bring this dimension of an "invisible" world into our own lives, and so discover a deeper sense of meaning and purpose. Through her many personal experiences and narratives, Balega reminds us that these glimpses into a mystical consciousness are available to us all and reflect primordial beliefs in an afterlife following death.*

Dr. Annamaria Hemingway, author of *Practicing Conscious Living and Dying* and *Myths of the Afterlife*

Betsy is a wonderful and kind hearted person. Who uses her talent to help others, in a positive manner. We need more folks like Betsy.

Maria Cheung, Special Event Co-Ordinator, The Hudson Bay Company, Toronto, Canada

If you believe in God - Betsy's book will deepen your faith & spiritual discernment. If you don't believe in God - the book could change your heart & mind!

Cher Chevalier Author, *The Hidden Secrets of A Modern Seer*

Betsy's book sparkles from the first page. You can't help seeing through her physical eyes and her sixth sense as she describes her childhood in Shamokin, Pennsylvania. This book will open your spiritual heart!

Dr. Laurie Nadel Author, *Dr. Laurie Nadel's Sixth Sense: Unlocking Your Ultimate Mind Power*

Acknowledgments

I would like to thank everyone at O-Books for their acceptance, help, advice and support. Thank you especially to John Hunt, Trevor Greenfield, Stuart Davies, Nick Welch and Sarah Dedman.

Psalms and Bible verses are from the Catholic Public Domain Bible.

Dedication

For God and Francis

Introduction

Some of you reading this may know me. Some of you may be old friends, and others may know me from my internet show, *Tuning in with Betsy*. Some of you may never have heard of me. All of you may be wondering why I wrote this book. The answer is simple. I am questioned, all the time, by people who want to know when I started *doing this*, why they should believe anything I say, how old I was when I first began to have visions and see dead people and how they can learn to do what I do. It is also for those people who think clairvoyants and mediums have an easy life with no problems. They believe we go through life with all the answers and no heartbreak. Nothing could be further from the truth.

It's for the people who ask me if I believe in God. Yes, I do. It's for people who tell me I have a gift. We all have gifts. I consider my ability to prophesy one of the nine gifts of The Holy Spirit; ergo I am not in league with demons or their boss. It's for those who have asked if they can be my apprentice. No, you can't, go see Donald Trump; he's in the apprentice business, not me. It's for people who have asked if I do spells. No, I don't perform spells, or cast curses on people. I pray often and have received phenomenal answers to those prayers. It's especially for people who want to do what I do. You can. This book should answer your questions and more. It is intended to be a book of hope and guidance for you.

The personal experiences I relate to you in this book are not meant to inflate my own self-importance but to share spiritual lessons I have learned. Some names have been changed to respect and protect the privacy of the individuals involved. Hopefully, as you apply prayer and meditation in your daily life, you too will have numerous supernatural stories of your own to share some day. As you read, and take the short exercises to heart, meditate and pray, I expect you to develop a much stronger connection with God and be in touch with Him. You'll feel your spiritual shift into the mystic and never want to go back. If you're ready, let's begin.

Chapter 1

In The Beginning

It was the best of times. I was young, free to do whatever I liked, as long as I stayed on my block, in my backyard, or next door, playing with the neighbor kids. The worst that could happen to me, in my four–year-old mind, was having only four cents for a five cent popsicle. Somehow that fifth penny always turned up in the little house my parents rented on Gowan Street, in my hometown, Shamokin, Pennsylvania.

Don't Google Shamokin for any great business mergers or takeovers. You won't find any. Forget great corporations rising from Shamokin. You won't find them either. What you will find is a small, third class city nestled in the Pennsylvania Coal Region. People there have solid values, kind hearts, and think Joe Paterno walks on water, or at least on real grass.

This was my 'hood. It was safe, friendly and fun. My grandparents lived two blocks away. My school was at the top of my street, and Unger's Drugstore, with a wide selection of penny candy, was at the bottom. What more could a four-year-old want? It didn't take much to keep me happy. Dick Clark, hosting *American Bandstand* from Philly every afternoon, made my day. It didn't get better than this, but something was happening outside of the television box. Every so often, I would experience knowing things before they happened. I *saw* things before they happened. It was like having a movie screen play inside my head with trailers of upcoming events. I didn't know anything about a third eye; I was just happy if I didn't lose the ears belonging to my Mr. Potato Head.

That October, when I was four, I kept seeing snapshots in my mind of being dressed as a cartoon character for Halloween. I

3

had no control over these images; they happened spontaneously. I saw myself visiting my grandparents with my family and trick or treating around the neighborhood dressed as a panda bear. I had no such costume. As Halloween advanced, the visions of me wearing a Miranda Panda costume increased. Several days before Halloween, my mother came home with a box containing one Miss Miranda Panda Halloween outfit for me to wear. How did Mom do that? I wondered. I had not told her what costume to buy and I had kept silent regarding the pictures I had seen of me in the panda outfit.

That was the beginning. Mom and I would share this unspoken telepathic connection for a lifetime. It was the beginning of a life filled with visions, voices, intuition, the sixth Sense, ESP, angels, prophetic dreams, happy visions, sad visions, a voice telling me in high school that my girlfriend would die within the week, seeing friends and relatives come and go, marrying, divorcing, having children, losing children and more. It was something I could not control. It would be years later, in my twenties, when I learned how to focus and channel this ability in psychic development classes with an astute teacher. At age four, I was just thrilled to be Miranda Panda for a few days.

I didn't know the process, or how this knowing in advance worked. All I knew was that whatever *it* was that *showed* me my costume, it was right. I liked that, but was puzzled because I didn't know the why and how of it. I assumed this knowing ahead of time, was part of life. I erroneously assumed everyone saw things beforehand all the time. Everyone knows all about it, I thought. That's why they don't talk about it. It's normal. I guessed my parents would explain it to me once I was old enough to go to school. I didn't have time to worry over it, I was too busy playing and having fun. Did it scare me? No, it gave me a sense of wonder about the world. It still does. I didn't know anything about energy, coincidences, or synchronicity. I knew something was going on in my life but I had no name for it. It was real. It was a mystery. It was a real mystery to my young mind. Whatever *it* was, *it was always right*. The amazing accuracy of this mystery was what fascinated me the most.

Freedom ended when I entered first grade at St. Edward Elementary School. It was time to get serious about the Three R's and my parents still hadn't explained to me how knowing things in advance worked.

My teacher was an Immaculate Heart of Mary (IHM) sister, by the name of Sister Mary Edward. What I loved most about her was that she told the most wonderful stories. She shared true stories about guardian angels, saints and miracles with the class. These were right up my alley. I wondered if Sister Mary Edward ever knew things ahead of time too. She seemed to have a steady supply of these fascinating supernatural stories that enthralled me. She had stories of angels helping people out when things seemed hopeless. Those were my favorites. The angels always came through with the right answers to solve the problems for the people. Her stories emphasized hope. She told stories about believers one-upping non-believers. The non-believers had earthly power. The believers triumphed at the end of each story with God's power.

I loved this nun and her stories so much that she became the recipient of my six-year-old venture into philanthropy. Every Monday I'd visit sister at lunch time and give her the weekly allowance that my parents had given me on Saturday. She reciprocated by giving me small trinkets as a thank you. It was easy for me to give up twenty-five cents worth of candy in exchange for a lamb sticker from sister, or a spool of forest green ribbon which I had no particular use for. (The color forest green would show up in my life later as a huge hello from God.) Sister taught me to give and receive. It was a good lesson from a great teacher.

Then it happened: Sister was teaching us how to write capital letters. I had made progress with the first eight letters of the alphabet, but that ninth letter was like the Sphinx smirking at me. I just couldn't grasp the technique of writing a capital 'I'. After handing in a full page of the letter, I knew what was coming my way. I didn't need a third eye to see it. There was no need for a vision to show me the obvious. There was no way out of this situation. The handwriting was on the blackboard or it was about to be. And it would be mine. I knew once sister saw my page, which looked like a combination of hieroglyphics and an alien alphabet, Elizabeth Balega would be called up to the front of the classroom to demonstrate how to write a proper capital I. Elizabeth Balega was about to fail in front of the entire class. How humiliating.

What could be worse than this? I would be embarrassed in front of all my friends and classmates. Humiliation and shame awaited me at the front of the room. I was filled with dread and fear. Within a few minutes, Sister Mary Edward called out as expected, 'Elizabeth Balega, go up to the blackboard.' My worst fear had come upon me. Move over Job, make room for me; you're about to have company. What could I do? I knew I wasn't able to learn how to make the letter 'I' correctly on my way up to the blackboard in ten seconds. I had struggled with it for twenty minutes at my desk. There was no hope. I could not write capital 'I' and I knew it. The entire class was soon to find out my shameful truth. I was stupid. I remembered sister's stories of guardian angels, ever ready to help us when we needed them. I needed mine now. Getting up from my seat I said a quick silent prayer, 'Guardian angel, help me. I am about to be embarrassed in front of everyone.'

Once I reached the blackboard, as I had expected, sister requested that I show the class how to write the capital letter I. As I reached for the chalk, something supernatural happened. Someone, an invisible someone, my angel, grabbed my right hand, lifted it, and wrote the most perfect capital I that Sister Mary Edward, or anyone, had ever seen. I don't know who was more shocked, Sister Mary Edward, or me. I knew my guardian angel had heard my silent plea to get me out of the mess I was in. He answered without hesitation. From that moment forward I knew that I would never be alone in life. God had sent an angel to watch over me at birth. He came to my rescue in the classroom that day and we would be going through life together. What a friend! Sister simply said, 'Thank you, Elizabeth. You may sit down.' That was the beginning of a beautiful friendship. My guardian angel came through. He has done many more favors for me throughout the years. The gratitude I felt that day in first grade forged a bond that will never break.

The visions and knowledge of the future continued throughout the school year. In August, my grandfather and I were sitting on our favorite rocker on his front porch, chatting. He held me on his lap and said, 'When you graduate from eighth grade, I am going to buy you a gold watch.' Suddenly, my mood turned to one of sadness. Sadness because, as he told me the future as he saw it, I *saw* it in a different way. I had a vision that he would not live to see me graduate from St. Ed's. In fact, he was going to ride the Glory Train home a lot sooner than he or anyone in the family could realize. Once more my ability proved to be accurate. My grandfather died two weeks later. This was the first time knowing the future in advance foretold a sad event. Unfortunately, it would not be the last.

After my grandfather crossed over I still sensed him around me. I would smell his pipe tobacco, or think I heard him call me by my Hungarian nickname. At night I dreamed I was with him. We were as happy as we ever had been when he was on earth. I did not know about astral travel, but felt my dreams were real and more than just dreams. Something extraordinary was happening to me. To see my pappy again, all I had to do was go to sleep. I loved it.

Then one day he appeared in my bedroom. I wasn't frightened at all. He smiled and said, 'Bingo.' To hear that one word meant the world to me. It was a simple word but so significant. The previous Christmas my sister had received a bingo game as a present. Christmas night, everyone received their playing cards and the bingo began. I asked for my card to join in the fun, but was told by my parents I was too young to participate. My sister agreed that I would never understand the concept of bingo. It was my pappy who allowed me to sit beside him that night and learn how to play Bingo. He had the patience to explain the game to me and I caught on quickly. More than that, he made me feel included.

Here he was now, almost a year later, in spirit, recalling the night that had been so special to me. After giving me his one word message, he vanished in front of my eyes. A strange coincidence began to occur after his visit. At every family or parish bingo game I have ever attended since that day, I have felt my pappy beside me in spirit. Amazingly, I have consistently won the last prize at each game. It has been our special secret, an inside joke, between us all these years. Big jackpots don't entice me. I'm not the gambling type. It's the sweet simplicity of those manifestations, with very inexpensive prizes, that lift my heart and make me happy to know that my first bingo experience and an old fashioned Christmas was remembered on The Other Side of Life.

In second grade, I learned that a very important historical event had taken place in Shamokin. Shamokin was important after all. I was impressed because my church, St. Edward, was the first public building in the United States to be wired with electric lights. Thomas Edison himself had been there in 1873. The great inventor stood in the same church where I received my First Holy Communion. It might as well have been God Himself saying, 'Let there be Light,' instead of Edison flipping a light switch. Edison had made quite the impression on me as a seven-year-old.

Two decades later I would learn that his parents were

Spiritualists. I would also learn that when he was facing a problem in his laboratory and was stumped finding a solution, he would relax, go into the meditative state, and place a pair of ball bearings in the palms of his hands. He would tune into the Universal Intelligence for a few minutes. By the time Edison had relaxed and the ball bearings fell to the floor, he woke up with the answer he had been searching for. His problem was solved. He was in tune and in touch with a Higher Power; a Higher Power that always answered without fail. You have access to this same Higher Power today and will learn how to tune in for yourself in later chapters.

Third grade was taught by Mrs. Shegon. She introduced us to Our Lady of Fatima and her predictions from 1917, when she appeared to three children in Fatima, Portugal. These predictions proved to be uncannily accurate and piqued my interest in End Time prophecies.

By now my glimpses into the future were happening more frequently. One Friday evening, my family went downtown for our usual routine of shopping, paying bills and then enjoying dinner together. That evening, my mother took my sister into the Montgomery Ward Department Store while I stayed with Dad in the car. It was a quiet night in Shamokin, nothing to do but watch the shoppers as they walked by and read my comic book till Mom was finished. I noticed an elderly man across the street. He was standing at the red light, waiting for it to turn green so he could cross Independence Street. Suddenly, I heard a voice speak to me: 'That man is going to walk by the car, and when he gets to the rear window, he is going to toss in some red and white striped peppermint candy. He will say, 'I have lots of candy like this for nice little boys and girls like you.' He will then go speak to your father, even though he doesn't know him. He will stand at the front passenger seat window and talk to your dad until your mother and sister return from the store.'

Here it was again. Somehow, I was going into the future once more. This time it was an invisible being telling me of an upcoming event, albeit an insignificant one in my opinion. Stranger still were the exact details of the message. Why was I being told about this little scenario? I wasn't sure it would happen. Why should I believe this voice? I had no connection to the old man. Why would he bother to give me candy? He didn't know me. And who was this disembodied voice? Was it my guardian angel? I guessed it was. A small bit of doubt crept into my mind. We'll see, I thought. That old man means nothing to me. Why should he care to toss candy in the car for me when he will never see me after he shuffles past? He doesn't know my dad. Why would he stop and talk with a complete stranger? It didn't make any sense to me whatsoever. And there is no little brother in the back seat with me. Why would he mention little boys when I am a girl? He is so bent over he can barely raise his head. He probably won't even see me as he walks by, he is so stooped. He is so slow a snail could beat him across the street. Mom and Michele will be back before he gets here. We'll be long gone. My logical mind had reasoned the old man out of my life.

I read my comic book, listened to the radio, and joked with Dad. I had forgotten all about the crippled old man. Mom sure was taking longer than usual in the store. It had never taken her this long before. What was taking her so long tonight? I wondered. Suddenly, there he was. The old crippled man was walking by my rear window. Wow, he's slower than molasses in January, I thought. It took him about half an hour to get to the car. I shouldn't be criticizing him. If I was in my eighties I guess I would walk as slowly as him. He was almost past the rear passenger window. I began to mentally congratulate myself that I had been right about the mysterious voice not knowing what he was talking about. I reached for my comic book when a handful of red and white striped peppermint candy came through the open window. The old man looked directly at me and said, 'I have lots of candy like this for nice little boys and girls like you.' I was speechless, but he wasn't. He just about crawled to the front passenger window and talked with my dad until Mom and Michele returned. Although it was a very insignificant incident, I knew someone was trying to get my attention. They certainly got it that evening in downtown Shamokin. I wondered what would be revealed next.

Looking back, I think my angel was preparing me, starting out with small events like this to prepare me to believe him when I would be told of bigger events on a larger scale. After this revelation, I happened to be watching television one Saturday afternoon and came across a show featuring ESP. Eureka! I was elated to learn that there were people doing experiments at Duke University, in New York City, Virginia Beach and in research centers around the world in precognition and telepathy. I was relieved, happy, overjoyed, and ecstatic that I now had a name for this ability. I realized it was no accident that I found that particular television show that day. Timing is everything and it was time for me to learn more.

My friend, Mary Pavone, came by a few Saturdays later. We couldn't decide what games to play that afternoon, so I suggested we play ESP. I thought this was my chance to discuss ESP and compare stories with her and my sister, Michele. Mary and my sister asked me what ESP was. 'It's when you know what things are going to happen before they happen,' I explained. Up until that day, I had still assumed this natural knowing was part of life and every person had experiences like mine. Didn't Mary, Michele and every kid in Shamokin see the future and hear angel voices like me? I learned the answer to that question that day. It was no. I was disappointed that they had no idea what I was talking about.

By the age of nine, I was happy to learn that there were people like me who lived a long time ago. I wasn't alone after all. They also had visions of the future. Their batting averages were untouchable; they had a 100% accuracy rate. Their names were Isaiah, Jeremiah, Ezekiel, and Daniel. I learned about them in fourth grade when Sister Joseph Therese (now known to all of her St. Ed's kids as Kathy Ianelli since leaving the religious life) taught the Old Testament. I couldn't get enough of these prophets. They were amazing and accurate. They were never wrong. Of course, they were in touch with God, so failure wasn't an option. When you stay in touch with Him you don't fail.

On Friday afternoons, after school, when Mary and the other kids on Franklin Street were outside playing, I would be in my parent's bedroom reading the Bible. Yes, I was reading the Old Testament. I had found kindred souls, even if they had been dead for thousands of years. I wanted to know more about them. I wished I could be more like them. My concern was who in the world would ever listen to me when these infallible experts, God's prophets, were ignored. The important thing was for me to stay close to God. I was to obey Him, read His Word, pray, trust and believe Him. I knew at a young age, my path in life would be a spiritual one. I knew I wasn't headed to Wall Street. Futures were in my future, but they were going to be other people's futures. I was to use my gift from the Holy Spirit to help people.

For the most part, this young seer was good at heeding my guardian angel, except for one time when I chose to ignore him. It was an experience I'd never forget. I disobeyed my mother and my angel on the same day. That was a big mistake. My sister and my friend Gail were attempting to teach me how to ride a two wheel bike. My mother told me not to go riding any bikes that afternoon. Yeah, yeah, I hear you, Mom, I thought, but this is my chance to learn how to ride a two wheeler. It's time for me to grow up.

At age nine, I had my own agenda for the day. After rushing past my mother, I heard the voice of my guardian angel very clearly say, 'Obey your mother.' Later angel, I'm busy. I am going to learn how to ride a bike today. One disobedient act is just a venial sin. It's no big deal. I can wipe out the stain later today with the Act of Contrition and some penance prayers from Father Lavelle in the confessional.

The three of us girls decided it was time for me to hone my bike riding skills. What better time was there than now? Within twenty minutes, I was wobbling on the back of Gail's bike. Suddenly a car appeared out of nowhere on our one way street. Gail swerved, deciding it was safer to crash into a parked car instead of a moving one. Dr. Al Schiccatano booked an emergency dental appointment that afternoon. Who was his patient? I'm sure you've guessed correctly. It was me. Did I learn a lesson that day? Yes, I did. When you get orders from your mother and a message from your guardian angel, listen and obey both of them. I had lots of time to read the Bible. I was grounded. That was the last time I ever believed Betsy knew best.

The best thing about fifth grade was that Sister Angela Mary had more supernatural stories, like Sister Mary Edward's, to share with the class. My favorite was the story about the priest who had a close, prayerful personal relationship with his guardian angel. When friends scoffed at his claims, the father decided to prove his point. He asked his angel, out loud, to please bring a prayer book to him. The book was on a table across the room. When the prayer book arose and floated across the room into the priests' hands, his friends had a change of heart. They never made fun of the father and his angel again.

Sister taught us that our angels had their own names but since we did not know their true name it was okay for us to give our angel a name of our own choosing. Our angels would understand. That was the day my heavenly companion became Francis, whether he liked it or not. As a child, I had always been fond of the name Frances. Since I had been baptized Elizabeth, my angel would now be known as the Francis I had wanted to be. I assumed he'd like the name. He was in good company; there was Francis of Assisi, Francis Xavier and Frances de Sales (the patron saint of writers). Someday, when he defends me before God, I'll know his true name but until then he'll always be My Francis.

A week before I submitted this manuscript to O-Books, someone stopped by my home to chat with me concerning his development. He wanted me to tell him his guardian angel's name and the name of his spirit guide. He was worried that he was meditating in the wrong way. I assured him that there is no wrong way to meditate. I told him to choose a name for his angel that appealed to him, just like I had named Francis when I was ten. I heard the name Georgia as the name of his spirit guide.

My friend was shocked by my words. He told me he had chills. He revealed to me that he had named his guardian angel, George, when he was nine years old. Well, I told him, it's no accident but only natural that his guide was a female named Georgia. George and Georgia are his companions throughout this life. That's how the universe works. It was confirmation for him that he is communicating with his angel and his guide and is advancing on his spiritual path in the right direction at the right tempo. If you haven't named your angel yet, don't ask someone else to do the honors, choose the name you are inspired to give him or her. Nurture this special relationship daily.

Sixth grade was taught by Sister Marita Catherine. One of her sayings that confused me was, 'Time is so slow in Shamokin.' I didn't understand her reasoning. I used to think, *Sister, if it is 1 o'clock in Shamokin, it is also 1 o'clock in Philadelphia, and don't you understand that?* I was not about to challenge a nun, especially a nun from South Philly. Sister introduced us to the mystical Irish monk, St. Malachy. I am sure many of you know of his eerily accurate papal prophecies. He has named each pope, through verses describing their coat of arms, ancestry or a symbol that would identify them upon their election to the papacy. He's Ireland's answer to Nostradamus.

According to his prophecies, there would be one hundred

and sixteen popes from his time (the 12th Century) to the End Time. Sister shared St. Malachy's prophecy, of Ireland going beneath the sea seven years before Judgment Day, after which, Christ will return to earth and set up His kingdom, ushering in an age of peace. (The reason for the watery demise of Ireland is said to be to deprive the Antichrist of ruling the Irish faithful when he comes to power and rules the entire world.) She definitely had my attention with that prophecy, but when I pressed sister for more predictions about the future she did not want to discuss them. I think she feared giving me information overload. I was disappointed, but knew she had her reasons. For those of you who are curious, there will be only one pope after Benedict XVI. He will be Peter II.

My psychic ability took a big leap, when I had a dream in October 1963. In my dream, I was walking up Shamokin Street on a Friday afternoon. All the kids had been let out of St Ed's early for some reason. I wasn't sure what the reason was. Sadness permeated my dream. In it, my next door neighbor, Violet Dudeck, was driving home from work earlier than usual. She stopped her black and white Mercury to give me a ride home. She turned to me in the car and said, 'We don't have a president anymore.' Unfortunately, my dream came true on Friday November 22, 1963. That afternoon, while walking home early from school, after news of the assassination resulted in an early school dismissal, Violet pulled up beside me and offered me a ride home. As we sat in her car, listening to the news on the radio, she turned to me and said, 'We don't have a president anymore.' It was the end of innocence, or what passed for and was called innocence, in America.

The Washington D.C. seer, Jeane Dixon, had a premonition of our 35th President dying in office, back in 1956. She knew she could not stop it. There have been times in my life when I have seen things which I knew I could not stop. You will read about them in later chapters.

By fourteen, I had discovered the paranormal book section at the Shamokin Library. I devoured books, by Harold Sherman, Hans Holzer, the prolific Brad Steiger, Jeane Dixon and Ruth Montgomery. It was comforting to know ESP and visions were happening everyday to everyday people, like me. I wasn't alone. I wasn't the only person having visions that came true. If only I lived somewhere other than Shamokin, where I could connect with others to guide and teach me and exchange notes. That would happen in about ten years' time when I would move to Philadelphia.

In high school, I had close friends but didn't discuss ESP or the paranormal with any of them. We were too busy concentrating on boys, sports, school trips, dances, and school work. A girlfriend of mine was earning extra spending money by selling Avon. I earned my spending money by babysitting my three Godchildren on the weekends.

One Monday afternoon, my friend Michelle and I stayed late after school to help one of the nuns clean. Michelle gave me one of her Avon booklets to browse through. I ordered a few items. She wrote out my order and said, 'You don't have to pay me till Tuesday, not tomorrow, but next Tuesday when the orders come in.' I was about to say, 'Okay,' when I heard a voice say, 'You will never have to pay her any money, because she is going to die on Sunday in a car accident with a man.'

I was speechless. I was stunned. I had an eerie feeling. I didn't want to believe what I had just heard. 'Okay. Next Tuesday is fine,' I answered, as if everything was perfect and I had not heard the voice. In my heart of hearts I didn't believe I would ever pay for my Avon products. The voice that guided me and revealed future events had never been wrong in thirteen years. I was hoping this would be the exception to his accuracy. All I could do was wait and see what would happen on Sunday. I never told Michelle about the voice I had heard. I gave her no warning. I didn't mention it. If I had told her she would have thought that I was off my rocker. She'd think I was crazy to believe in a mysterious voice. I did not believe I could change this event if it was going to happen. It was outside of my control. I kept quiet.

That Sunday, my parents and I took a drive to the Pennsylvania Grand Canyon. We left home before noon and headed north. All day I had an overpowering sense of sadness surrounding me. It was an atmosphere of grief but I didn't know why I was feeling so emotional. I was ready to cry at any moment. I could not for the life of me figure out why I was feeling so melancholy. I could not shake the sense of sadness and the readiness to shed tears.

That evening, we arrived home and heard the news that my friend, Michelle, had died that day around noon on route 61. Her father's car had been hit broadside while exiting a shopping mall. She had died instantly. The voice had been right again. This message had been more serious than the one about an old man crossing the street and sharing peppermint candy with me. Why hadn't I said something? Why hadn't I warned her? 'If only' are the two saddest words in any language. If only I had warned my friend she would still be alive. I spoke with my mom about the voice that had revealed my friend's fate. She listened to me but had no ready answer or explanation for it. I thought of talking with our school principal, but didn't think he would understand and so I remained silent.

Over the years I have discussed this incident with priests, ministers and mediums. They all agreed unanimously that there was nothing I could have done to change Michelle's destiny. I have learned that there is a day and time we come into this world and a day and a time when we leave it. I could not have changed my friend's destiny. Fate can include sad twists. The happy twist to this story is that I went on to sit in development class and my friend Michelle has come to visit with me many times since we were in high school. God turned something sad into something good years later.

Moon Over Miami

Visiting Disneyland was on my bucket list for seventeen years when, lo and behold, Uncle Walt was opening Disney World in the Sunshine State. I was ready for a vacation especially one where I could act like a kid again at the ripe old age of twenty. A friend and I set off in October to visit the Magic Kingdom. We stayed with his aunt and uncle in West Palm. Having such a grand time on vacation, I decided I should move to Florida permanently and enjoy the wonderful weather all year long.

Before I made my move south, I would attempt to immigrate to Canada. Another dream vacation, the prior year, had ignited a strong desire in me to live north of the 49th Parallel. Off went my request to Ottawa. Back came Ottawa's reply. It was an official application asking to know how much property I owned. It asked what my portfolio included and the amounts in my bank accounts. They assumed I had accounts. I had an account but it wasn't about to impress Immigration Canada. I wondered if Ottawa had ever seen so many zeroes on an application before. Canada would have to wait; I was headed south. Moving to Florida would be so much easier than moving to a new country and the compass of my life was pointing southeast.

To prepare for my big move, I researched the City of Miami, via *the Miami Herald*. I bought the paper each weekend and studied the classifieds for opportunities. I felt it was not just time for a move, but also a career change. I decided the hospitality industry was going to be my new field of employment. There would be no more offices in my future. What better place to get started than Miami Beach? Hospitality personnel were in great demand. The hotels and clubs needed hostesses and waitresses who were outgoing, energetic, dedicated and possessed a great sense of humor. These ads definitely sounded like me. I applied to various establishments and anxiously waited for the replies to fill my mailbox.

Replies trickled in but no solid job offer materialized. However, my dream job jumped out at me from the pages of the classifieds when I saw an ad placed by Stuart X. Stuart X was the manager of one of Miami Beach's best and busiest clubs. He was in the market for hostesses and waitresses who could be trained. They needed to work a flexible schedule and naturally they had to possess that great sense of humor.

I replied to Mr. X's ad with what I considered to be a cordial letter of introduction. I explained to Stuart X that I was Sunshine-State-bound in approximately eight months. I would be an ideal employee and requested an interview. His reply arrived two weeks later, but it wasn't the reply I'd expected. It had a tone of arrogance to it and no interest in me whatsoever as an employee. He ended his curt letter with this sentence: 'Is there really life in Pennsylvania?' Ouch! I was nobody to him and not worth his time. I wasn't worthy of being one of his employees. I knew not all employers possessed his attitude. I was sure there were many other employers who were considerate, kind and caring down South, he just wasn't one of them.

As I held his mean spirited letter, I had a vision of Stuart X. I saw him getting into an Eldorado Cadillac, turning the ignition key, the car exploding, and his legs being cut off from the knees down. There was no voice accompanying this vision. I didn't need to hear a voice. I knew what Francis was telling me. His strong visual had been enough to get his message across. I needed to let go of any dream of ever working for this person. I needed to let go of my hurt feelings. I needed to let go of this letter *now*. Forgedaboutit! I did. Francis only had to show me once. The hurt dissolved, as if Jesus the Christ was beside me and had touched me. All was okay. Spirit, my Francis, was telling me to give it no more thought, time, energy or worry. How often he has guided me with explicit visions and has always proved to be correct.

I did move to Miami as planned and began work at a hospital. I lived in Coconut Grove, enjoyed my job, and had terrific friends in Miami. All was right in God's universe. One evening, I turned on the local ABC affiliate station in Miami. The leading news story featured one Mr. Stuart X who had his legs blown off in an explosion that afternoon when he turned the ignition key to start his Eldorado Cadillac. His legs, the journalist reported, were amputated from the knees down. All I could think was *Francis you showed me the truth last year. I will never doubt you. Thank you for keeping me away from him.* God had protected me. The truth always comes out. My fantastic Francis was right on point. Angels, God's messengers never lie. I always knew that. I would see Francis reveal the truth many times in the years to come.

Doctors and nurses at the hospital would tease me at work and say, 'Betsy, with your personality and energy you should be working at a hotel or club on Miami Beach.' I'd just smile and say, 'No, I am right where I am supposed to be.' God and Francis had warned me once; I didn't need to be warned twice. This experience made me realize I was to work with healers in a healing environment throughout my life.

Nowadays, it seems that becoming rich and famous (or rich and well known and not really having talent) is what many people chase after. In 2007, I asked someone what she had dreamed of as her career since childhood. She astounded me with her response, 'All I've ever wanted is to walk the red carpet.' Walking the red carpet is not a career. Only a handful of people win an acting award each year. Only a small percent of actors make it to the top in Hollywood. It was definitely time for a reality check for her, not a reality TV show.

Everyone has God given talents and a purpose that was given to them before they entered the earth this time around. It's your job to accept your talents and live a life filled with meaning. I am sure you have heard that the talents and abilities God gave you are God's gifts to you; what you do with them are your gifts to Him. How true that is.

God put me where He wanted me, comforting the sick and dying patients. Was it glamorous? No, it was not. Was it an east coast version of *Grey's Anatomy*? Absolutely, it was not. I was working nights, weekends, holidays and enjoying the days in Coconut Grove. The only negative aspect of life in The Grove was the high crime rate. It seemed the holidays were an invisible psychic signal sent out to criminals in the area to go break and enter into Betsy's apartment.

It began the first Christmas in Miami when I received a call from the Miami police telling me their SWAT team had my duplex surrounded. Welcome to Christmas in Miami! The next spring, burglars broke in and traipsed through my home on Easter Sunday morning, at 1 am as I slept. Did it get worse? Oh yes it did. The next Labor Day weekend, I met the burglar at my bedroom door at 4 am.

From that night forward, I kept all the lights on, pondered getting a Doberman as my new best friend and installing bars over all of the windows. You would think I would take God's hints and get out of Dade, ASAP. Mais non Francis, I stayed in The Grove. Moving became a yearly event to a more expensive street. Like the Orange Bowl, Mr. Blackwell's Worst Dressed List and the Philadelphia Mummers Parade, I could anticipate moving to a more expensive address with more security measures every year, after another holiday break-in. Ob La Di Ob La Da, life went on yeah.

B&Es were common, but the big news in Broward and Dade Counties, in my third year living in Miami, was a character named The Canal Killer. His M.O. was to abduct an unsuspecting female, take her to a remote area, sexually assault her, strangle her, dismember her lifeless body and leave a piece of the victim's jewelry on her body for her family to be able to identify her. The victims had been found in canals in the area, hence his moniker.

One night at work, a friend and I needed to add some ice to our ever present tumblers of water. The ice machine was located inside a room where bodies on the way to the morgue were sometimes temporarily kept. The room was adjacent to the medical side of the ER. It would take just a minute to grab some ice for our room temperature drinks. It would take a lifetime to erase the horror that met us on the other side of the door that night. There was the body of one of our friends and co-workers, who had become the latest victim of The Canal Killer.

Crime hit closer to home that night than I hope it ever does again. My friend had gone shopping and parked her car at a mall on Miami Beach. When she was finished her shopping, she came out to discover her car had a flat tire. A male approached her and offered assistance. He offered to drive her to a garage and her problem would be solved; he could have the tire replaced in no time. That was just a ploy to gain her trust and get her into his vehicle. Unbeknown to my friend, this person had flattened the tire himself. The time had come for me to say goodbye to Miami but not to my friend Ronnie. Our paths would cross a few years later in Canada. Just like Michelle, she comes to visit often.

The Philadelphia Story

Philadelphia was my next stop on my life's journey. My new home, with the approval of both parents, was a residence for young women in the heart of the City of Brotherly Love, which was managed (to their delight) by Dominican nuns. I loved being in the middle of Philly. Security was tight at the Lucy Eaton Smith Residence on Sansom Street. Good luck to the fool who would try messin' with a dozen nuns and two night security guards.

The residence had a strong spiritual vibration. I settled into my new home with ease. I made friends, enjoyed Fairmount

Park, The Philadelphia Art Museum, cheese steaks, hoagies, the Phillies, Flyers and Eagles. The vibration at the residence was one of another unworldly serenity. The hustle and bustle certainly existed outside the building but inside I felt a calm and peacefulness I had never experienced. I attributed it to the chapel on the mezzanine and the chief resident there. I would stop by almost every day to chat with God and tell Him what was going on in my life, as if I had to tell Him. He already knew.

At night, all was calm, for a while. After a few weeks, I awoke in the middle of the night to party sounds. I heard a piano playing, but not current songs. No, this music was more Scott Joplin's style. The voices, mainly female, were laughing and joking. They sure sounded happy. They definitely were not nuns. I felt like I was missing one terrific party from another era. Who were these nightly time traveling revelers? I had heard a variety of stories from my friends at the residence. The gossip was that the residence had once been a hotel with an intriguing history. I attempted to speak with Sister Margaret about these nightly noises, but she wasn't giving up any ghosts. Like Sister Marita Catherine, she chose to remain silent and not discuss the topic of spirits with me.

Then, as in 1934, it happened one night. I found myself standing beside my bed after I had gone to sleep hours earlier. I turned around and to my amazement there was a strand of silver light, a cord extending from my solar plexus connecting my astral body to my physical body. My physical body was on the bed. To my surprise, I couldn't have cared less about my physical body or what happened to it. The *real Betsy* was a spirit. I knew my real body was my spirit body, not the physical body lying on my bed.

Gee, living at this residence with the nuns certainly had benefits I never dreamed I would ever have. This first astral projection made having spirit partiers as nightly guests mundane. Being able to leave my physical body and have the freedom to explore the astral realms was an amazing experience. What an adventure. After popping out of my physical body, now what? What should I do? Where should I go? Should I be adventurous or stay close to home? Close to home won out. Instead of running off to the Eiffel Tower or the Grand Canyon (that would come years later), I decided I had better not push my luck and stayed inside the residence. I could go check things out downstairs and stop by and say hello to God in the chapel.

My astral stroll didn't last very long; after a few minutes of checking out the hallways and the chapel, I decided to return to my room. I didn't want to push my luck the first time out. Getting back into my body was easy. It went smoothly. I didn't land with that famous jolt we so often experience. I'm sure many of you have experienced jolting yourselves wide awake in the middle of the night. That is when you have returned from your sky walking/astral adventures and not executed a smooth landing. It happens to all of us, and is quite a common feature of astral projection.

I didn't share stories of my astral travel excursions with anyone, until I felt comfortable enough to confide in my friend, Angie, another resident at 1929 Sansom Street. To my relief, she did not think I was out to lunch, nuts or delusional. She listened attentively. Weeks later, she shared a similar story with me of how she had found herself up in the corner of the ceiling of her room one night, only to look down and see her physical body sound asleep on her bed. She traveled inside the residence and ventured outside once she felt comfortable.

Any fear of death that we might have had disappeared completely. We knew without a doubt that we survive death because we were having these astral experiences on a regular basis. My physical body will decay some day but my body of light is eternal. With my friend sharing her experiences we became kindred spirits and closer than ever. By this time I was beginning to think that not only are we all capable of out of body travel but the spiritual vibration of the residence was speeding up my innate psychic ability. Dreams of the future were happening almost nightly. I would dream of an event and the event would come true the next day or within a week at the latest.

I've always been an avid radio fan. As my psychic experiences continued to escalate, I just 'happened' to turn on the radio one evening to find Sid Mark hosting a show with a Philadelphia clairvoyant by the name of Valerie Morrison. I didn't believe that finding the show was just a coincidence. It was meant to be. Every Wednesday night, between 7 and 9 pm, Valerie would take questions from callers and answer them with her clairvoyant ability. Try as I might, I was never one of the lucky listeners to get through to her. The only thing for me to do was to book a private reading with Valerie. My reading with her was the real deal.

The day before my appointment with Valerie, I had gone shopping on Chestnut Street in Philadelphia. I had bought a pastel dress to wear to work at Thomas Jefferson University Hospital. It was mid-February and not the season for pastels but I didn't care. Pastels were and still are my favorite colors to wear. I believe colors affect our moods. Pastels uplift my mood and I still wear them in winter. I felt it was the right purchase for me no matter what season it was or what the fashion magazines touted. Of course, Valerie confirmed it was the right purchase for me the next night.

As I sat down in Valerie's office she remarked, 'Betsy, pastels are for you. Wear lilac, blues, pinks, white and pale greens no matter what the season. Your vibration is not for dark colors. Wear pastels.' Had this woman been astral traveling into my closet? The dress I had bought the day before was lilac. That was the first color she had mentioned. To this day, I've yet to own that classic little black dress. You won't find it at my house. I never felt drawn to that *Breakfast at Tiffany's*, Audrey Hepburn

25

iconic dress. That was meant for other women to wear, not me. Valerie confirmed what I already knew. She confirmed a lot more, telling me I was a natural born psychic and should now sit in psychic development classes. It was time to focus and direct my natural abilities. She also made a remark that absolutely stunned me. She casually mentioned that I had been a nun in a past life in France. I had begun to study French at age nine in my current life. Could that be just a coincidence too? The religious sisters from my lifetime in France would visit me in Toronto seven years later.

Aside from reassuring me about my fashion sense, Valerie did me the biggest favor of all by introducing me to her friend, medium Mary Polis. By April, I was sitting in class with Mary and eleven other students. Each Monday night, Mary would teach us how to meditate, tune in, focus our abilities and act responsibly. She taught us psychometry, how to connect with our healing angels, how to see auras, tap into past lives, remote view, and how to send absent healing. My grandfather, who had passed eighteen years earlier, came through to connect with me in our circle. How I looked forward to those Monday night classes.

Many people have asked me over the years, 'Betsy, when did you know you were a good clairvoyant?' My answer has always been the same. It was the night in class when we learned psychometry. We exchanged a piece of jewelry with another classmate and read from the vibration of the jewelry. Holding their ring, or watch, we were to name the style of the person's house, their favorite color, whether the person we were reading had a cat or a dog, and what their favorite type of music was.

As I held my classmate's wedding ring I kept seeing Montreal and a fishing boat. The vision would not go away. Instead of fading away, the images of Montreal became stronger and stronger. I saw St. Joseph's Oratory, the St. Lawrence River, and Notre Dame Cathedral. This was definitely Montreal. When it was time to give the information to our partners, I told mine the style of house she owned, her cat's name, her favorite type of music, her favorite color then added my vision of Montreal with the boat. I expected ridicule but instead got confirmation from her. Her husband was leaving the next morning at 4 am to go on a fishing trip to Montreal, Quebec. It was that night I knew never to doubt whatever I am shown by my angel, no matter how unusual it might seem. As you develop remember this. Go with what you are shown and do not doubt it. You may receive information you were not asking about but there is always a reason why it is being given to you. Learn to trust your angels, guides, God and yourself.

There is a saying that spirit never lies. Mary taught us to always go with what we first saw in meditation. Do not try to be logical. She was right. Many times people think their future must follow a logical course. When their life takes a surprising turn they panic. That is the best time to remember God is in control. He may have other plans for you and your life; plans that you are not yet aware of.

I have a friend who had the intention of opening an event planning company four years ago and now is headed to nursing school in January. My friend is more excited about becoming a nurse than she ever was about owning a business. During your most confusing times it's vital for you to remain calm and not panic. Don't think the worst, like Job; you know what happened to him. He is the prime example of the power of your mind to attract and bring exactly what you don't want into your life. It can be difficult and a challenge to remain positive in a negative world, but that's exactly what you must do. As you go into the mystic, practice patience, prayer and meditation. Stand on His Word. Remember His promises. Call on Him. Connect with Him and you'll see wonderful things come to pass.

Chapter 2

Toronto the Good

If Philadelphia, and meeting Valerie Morrison and Mary Polis, was boot camp, Toronto has been my spiritual tour of duty. Toronto has given me the opportunity to sit in class with some of the best mediums at the Britten Memorial Spiritualist Church. I continued my studies, in Toronto, where I had left off in the City of Brotherly Love. It wasn't difficult to find the Toronto Public Library; there are ninety-eight branches plus the Toronto Reference Library. The paranormal book section, at my branch, was triple the size at the library in my hometown.

I have always thought that February was a special time from God, a month with snow, cold temperatures and early sunsets to give us more time to read. Once again, it was no accident that, in the month of February, I came across a book, which mentioned the oldest Spiritualist church in Toronto. The Britten Memorial Spiritualist Church had been incorporated in 1926 and is located in Toronto's West End. My logic reasoned if this church has been in Toronto since 1926, and the mediums have not been run out of town on a rail by now, they must be authentic. I just had to go, at least once, and see what a service was like. My initial visit occurred on Valentine's Day at the afternoon message service.

I arrived at the correct subway stop, walked outside, and proceeded to get lost. After retracing my steps and checking the address again, I found the Britten Memorial Spiritualist Church. I decided the last row was the right place for me. The seat right next to the door was perfect. If things got a bit too strange, or spooky, I could make a quick, quiet exit and be at the subway in a New York minute. On the contrary, nothing was strange or spooky about the church or the service. The mediums, and student mediums, were gracious and friendly.

I received a message from a young woman, Debbie J., who looked no older than twenty. I wondered what she was going to tell me. She brought through a young man from the Other Side wearing a United States Army Uniform. He was telling her that everyone in the family was surprised when he died. He admitted no one was more surprised than he was, when he found himself outside of his body and in another world. The quick transition, of being in the physical one minute and in the spirit the next, had caught him totally off guard, but he was adjusting slowly and getting acclimatized to the change. Then Debbie gave personal information to me that only my cousin (who had served in Vietnam in the United States Army) and I could have known.

I was quite impressed with her messages. Thus began my foray into Spiritualism. At the end of the service, the floral centerpiece was taken apart and all the women who had attended the service were given a rose. I still have the rose that was given to me that day in a place of honor in my home. It's a happy reminder of my first message service.

After the service, everyone headed downstairs for a cup of tea and dessert. The medium, Debbie J., who had brought my cousin through, approached me and began to apologize. She stated that she knew she was wrong, that my soldier was not American, but 'had to be from Canada or Great Britain.' No, I told her, she had been absolutely correct. My cousin was American, just like me. He had served in the U. S. Army and did a tour of duty in Vietnam. She had doubted the first vision she had and tried to be logical with her spirit greetings. Once more, she reminded me of what I had been taught in Philadelphia. Go with what you first see and trust it is accurate. Don't try to be logical.

One thing that pleasantly surprised me was how Spiritualism and mediums were accepted as normal and natural in Toronto.

Talking with the dead wasn't viewed as anything strange but taken seriously. I met more mediums each week at the services. One medium from Britten became my best friend. He remains my closest friend to this day. Ron S. helped my development along by calling me each night and exchanging messages over the phone with me. We still exchange messages nightly. Ron's has been the last voice I've heard before nodding off to sleep every night since 1982. I often tell him, if he crosses over first, I won't know what I'll do every night at 9 pm, but he had better return in spirit nightly to continue our chats.

Healing classes, known as the laying on of hands in the Bible, were also taught weekly. Instead of touching the physical body we worked through the auras of people sitting in the healing chairs. I witnessed some amazing results. People who had been using canes when they first began attending were completely healed in a few weeks. Others, who had suffered broken bones, mended much faster than their doctors expected. Yes, God answers prayers and He is still healing today. He never went out of business. His healing angels come through to help. Doctors and nurses in spirit, return to work with healers to continue the wonderful healing they practiced when they were on earth in their physical form.

Meeting Spirit Guides

I had heard of spirit guides and read books about them for several years. I had never tuned in to find out who my guides were. I was used to communicating with my Guardian Angel Francis, but I was about to find out that Francis had company. As I sat in class at Britten, I began to receive more spontaneous messages throughout the day.

I was never one to indulge in salads or take an interest in vegetarian diets. I was more the burger and fries type. Imagine my surprise when I kept hearing a female spirit telling me to, 'Go to a salad bar'. Had I attracted a nutritionist from the Other

Side? I ignored the voice and her constant messages. I was content with my diet. Why should some dead person come back to admonish me about my bad eating habits? Mind your own business, I thought. Let me eat what I like. Until that time, the only thing I ate that even remotely resembled a salad were croutons drowned in Thousand Island Salad Dressing. I preferred to leave all the lettuce in the world for people who enjoyed it, and hungry rabbits everywhere.

This spirit dietician was relentless. Her messages increased until I couldn't stand it anymore. I decided to give in and visit the salad bar of a well known fast food restaurant (known for their square burgers and named for the owner's daughter). I skipped the lettuce but loaded my plate with red beets, broccoli, cottage cheese, raw onions, corn, and mushrooms. I ate everything on my plate and went back for seconds. There, that should make you happy and shut you up, whoever you are. I sent that thought out to the spirit, who had been hounding me. Yes, I did top off my healthy lunch with one of their frozen chocolate ice cream desserts. After all the healthy veggies, I felt I deserved a Frosty.

That evening, as if in response to my obedience, the spirit of a woman appeared to me and identified herself as Rose, a dietician who had worked in hospitals back in the 1940s. She spoke not with words, but telepathically. She had come to me as a guide, to help me with my spiritual work on earth. I wasn't surprised to have attracted someone who had worked at a hospital. I had, and still have, many friends who work in Medicine. She told me she wasn't trying to be a nag, but wanted me to eat healthy, because when I did, I would be on a higher vibration to receive her messages. The meat I had been eating was not conducive to working with her. I understood. I apologized for my attitude and changed my diet. This wouldn't be the last time that I would apologize to a spirit friend and admit that they were right and I was wrong.

My next meeting with one of my guides was one afternoon, while cleaning the kitchen. I have always felt closeness and a connection with the Zulu Tribe of Africa. Don't ask me why, but I have felt a spiritual connection with the Zulus in this lifetime. My intention in the 80s was to stay in Canada, become a landed immigrant and eventually a Canadian citizen, but the uncertainty of not knowing if I would be accepted gave me a strong sense of insecurity. I used to think to myself, I need the strength of a Zulu Warrior to get through this process. It wasn't as if I was warring with Immigration Canada, I just wanted strength to get through the time it would take to become a landed immigrant. Some days I wondered if I would ever make it. My grandfather had been processed at Ellis Island in the early twentieth century in a few hours. This process would take me almost five years.

One Saturday afternoon, while cleaning up in the kitchen, I heard a voice – a strong male voice – say to me, 'I am Haiji. You will be very happy staying in Canada.' Did I just hear what I thought I just heard? No one appeared, but I sensed that Haiji just had to be a Zulu Warrior. I had been thinking of the Zulus so strongly at that time. Perhaps a Zulu in the spirit world was with me to give me the strength that I had been hoping and praying for.

I didn't need to wait long for the confirmation. The next day was Sunday and it was time to go to church for messages. Once a month, the church held mediums night, when three or four mediums would give messages to the attendees. One of the mediums working the platform that evening came to me with this message: 'There is a Zulu Warrior standing behind you. I will tell you his name. I will spell it for you, H-A-I-J-I. His name is Haiji. He is telling me you should not worry about the biggest issue that is concerning you at this time. You will stay in Canada for many years.'

I thanked her for the message. She did not have to spell his name, because there had been a rock band, back home when I was a teenager, named Haiji. Was it another coincidence? I think not. I think Haiji had been with me for longer than I realized. As a teenager I could not pick him up in spirit. I wasn't at the spiritual level that I was reaching through meditation and attending classes. I did not sense him around me but once more, in hindsight, I think Haiji was around for years before connecting with me in Toronto. At that time, I had been developing for seven years and it was getting easier to communicate through the Veil.

I did a lot of praying during this time, asking God for His guidance. As I prayed, I sensed not just one nun, but a group of nuns surrounding me, praying with me. I wondered if I had known these nuns in a past life. Were they the nuns Valerie had mentioned in my first reading? I sensed a strong French vibration with them. That couldn't be an accident, or another coincidence. Sure enough, that week when I went to church, the medium had a message for me again. This time she told me, 'Do you know, when you pray, there is a group of Catholic nuns who surround you? They pray along with you. You were with them in a past life in a convent in France and they have not forgotten you.' I had my Zulu warrior and former friends praying with me. My spirits lifted knowing I had friends helping me in prayer and sending me strength through the Veil. (A meditation to meet your spiritual guides is included in a later chapter.)

As I wrote this book, I was contacted by a woman I'll call Denise who had the spirit of a woman who had committed suicide in her house. The deceased spirit meant her no harm, but came to warn her to move on from a toxic relationship. The deceased woman had been dating this woman's current boyfriend a year earlier. It was an abusive relationship and drove her to end her life. She came back to save his new girlfriend from suffering the same fate. When Denise took the steps to break away from him, the departed spirit was able to move on in the spirit realm. The deceased woman was not

Denise's spirit guide, per se, but came in temporarily to guide her away from a bad situation. This is just one example of how concern and compassion are extended through the Veil to help us here on the earth.

Haunted Houses – Mine

Not only did I meet spirits at church, but also in the home I was sharing with two housemates. We rented a house in Toronto's Little Italy. This spirit was rather rambunctious, opening windows in the dead of winter (again no pun intended), erasing phone messages when we were expecting important calls. The television, stereo and our answering machine would turn off and on by themselves. One of my housemates was continuously woken up at 4 am when her mattress would begin to shake uncontrollably. Talk about sleep deprivation; none of us ever got a full eight hours of sleep.

One day, while putting my laundry away, I noticed some of my delicate items were missing (delicate, meaning my bras and underwear). Ever the funny girl, I commented, 'I guess our ghost is a cross-dresser.' That night, at 4 am, it was my bed that was shaking uncontrollably. Apparently, this ghost lacked a sense of humor and was not amused. After a heartfelt, 'I was only kidding,' my bed was stationary. The ghost went back to the front bedroom, his favorite haunt.

The three of us tolerated this unseen guest as best we could. While having a Friday night chat session, I could no longer keep the secret of my psychic ability from Tina and Natalie. It was time to come clean and tell them about my other worldly background. I was happy to hear Natalie share with us that her grandfather was the village reader back home in his native Portugal. Tina was a skeptic. She didn't believe I could give accurate readings and definitely did not believe I could chit chat with the dead. The dead were dead and that's all there was to it, was her opinion. That didn't hurt my feelings. Everyone is entitled to their own opinion. I love skeptics. I knew spirit would take care of everything. There was no need to worry. And then a male spirit arrived as if on cue. I asked if either of them had an old boyfriend named Tom. Tina said that was the name of her first boyfriend when she was sixteen. I told her he was standing beside her at the end of the sofa. Tom told me that he had committed suicide and was now sorry he had gone through with it. When I relayed this to Tina she confirmed that it was true. The look on her face told me her skepticism was dissolving. It never takes spirit long to come to my defense. Tom mentioned his sister Angela and asked Tina to pass a message along to her. Tina confirmed Angela was the name of Tom's sister.

Soon Tina wanted to hear more. How quickly her attitude had changed from being a complete skeptic to wanting to know more. Tom explained his reason for taking his own life, and admitted that it wasn't much of a reason. He had felt he could not live up to his father and step-mother's expectations of him. The pressure of college scared him so he opted out of life. In the spirit, he realized how his death had affected all the people in his life. He was truly sorry and asked for Tina's forgiveness. Tom was a very sensitive and gentle soul, not the kind of person, or spirit, who would be playing tricks on us, or waking us up in the middle of the night for some attention. He added, if he had it to do over again, he would make a different choice, and would have remained on earth to resolve his problems. He was holding out a red rose for Tina.

When told this bit of information, Tina began to cry. Tom used to bring her a red rose on every date. This was a lot of information for Tina to process. She knew I had not just made up this story. She was beginning to think that perhaps there was something to this life after death stuff. Of course there is. Different religions and cultures have proclaimed it for centuries and now that the Veil is thinning, it is easier for our loved ones to communicate with us.

The regret of committing suicide comes through in every reading when a friend or family member has taken their own life. In meditation I have learned that if the person had stayed on earth, their angels and guides would have worked with them and led them to find the solutions to their problems. If anyone you know is suffering depression, talking about suicide or making statements like, 'It would have been better if I had never been born,' the National Suicide Hotline is 1-800-273-TALK (8255) in the United States and 1-800-448-1833 in Canada.

Soon, it was time for one of our favorite holidays, Halloween. Since I had to work that night, I was unable to attend the party my housemates were throwing. The next day, All Saints Day, I returned home from work to find a business card taped to the front door. Another salesman looking to sell us something we don't need, I thought as I took the card from the glass. When I read, Lt. XXXX RCMP, all I could think was, 'Now what kind of party did I miss, that the RCMP were called in by our neighbors?' I was apprehensive and a touch afraid, but ready to face the music if party-goers had broken any laws the night before. I dutifully rang up the RCMP Officer. He wasn't aware of any crazy goings on at our house on Halloween. He hadn't come by about party damages. He had been by to inquire about the previous resident at our rented house, Mr. XXXX. I knew that name, not because I knew the person, but because there had been a murder on College Street the previous year in Toronto. Mr. XXXX was the alleged murderer.

As I spoke to the officer, the penny dropped. Now I knew who our restless ghost was. Of course it hadn't been Tom but the twenty-year-old Vietnamese youth, who was the murder victim at the hands of the previous tenant. I assured the officer, none of us gals knew the criminal. We had moved in long after he had moved out. That was the end of his inquiry. Afterwards, I lit candles and offered prayers for the repose of the soul of the young man, Mr. Nguyen. When his soul returned one night, I sent him into the Light. The nightly rumblings in the house stopped and the TV, radio and answering machine were back to functioning normally.

Spirit Filled Houses

The next house I lived in also had spirits. The most memorable one was the deceased father of my landlord. I had come to see a house located closer to my work in downtown Toronto. I decided the location was perfect, the neighborhood was great and I was ready to move in. The day I showed up with a series of post-dated checks, my new landlord began to tell me how the relationship between he and his late father had been strained.

I wondered why he was revealing such personal information to me. He had just met me last week. Maybe he needed to talk so I let him and I listened. As he spoke sadly, and with a sense of regret, I could feel the bad blood between the two. Suddenly, a man materialized behind him and I knew without a doubt this was his father. He began to tell me, telepathically, how sorry he was for all the earthly misunderstandings between him and his son. Since this was only our second meeting, I did not think it was appropriate for a new tenant to boldly say, 'Don't worry, your dad has changed. He's standing right behind you. He understands you much better now than when he was on earth.' There's a time and a place for everything and this was not the time or the place to talk to an atheist about life after death.

It was at this house on a frigid February day that I sat in prayer and meditation in the living room. Glancing up, I saw a figure of a Capuchin monk standing in front of me. It was Padre Pio. There was no mistaking him. Many of you may know of this Italian mystical monk, canonized by his friend, Pope John Paul II, in 2002. He is now known as St. Pio. Words weren't spoken. He stood before me for a short time and as quickly as he appeared, he vanished. I have prayed to St. Pio for over thirty years. He has answered me for over thirty years. I tell my friends to pray to St. Pio; he's faster than Federal Express. Why did he appear to me? I think it was to encourage me to keep praying and not stop, to keep on the narrow spiritual path. Padre Pio was able to read souls. He also was clairvoyant, communicated with his angels and he could bi-locate. He is a true mystic. I am honored and blessed that he came by for a visit. He's welcome any time.

Padre Pio was not the only holy man to appear in the living room. Once again, while meditating by the fireplace, I looked up and there was a Native American medicine man. I was getting used to seeing spirit, but he was not alone. He was sitting on top of his life-sized white horse. Seeing a life-sized person in spirit was one thing, but I was amazed at a spirit horse materializing. It caught me off guard. Never in a million years did I expect to see this shaman sitting atop his horse. I had been meditating and was at a deep level. I had come out of the meditative state and was wide awake. I had to rub my eyes because I couldn't believe what I was seeing, but I did believe it. The shaman gave me a blessing, smiled and, like Padre Pio, vanished into the ether. These apparitions gave me a new confidence and a strong sense of spiritual growth. I loved being guarded and guided by such highly spiritually advanced souls.

Another home with friendly spirits was the former Mt. Pleasant Baptist Church, on Balliol Street in Toronto. It was founded in the early twentieth century. It had been renovated and was owned by a spiritual healer/French professor from Moscow, Russia. Each morning at exactly 1:11am, a tall pure white spirit would come through my front door. I used to joke with friends that he must be the caretaker of the church watching over me. I don't think the time he made his entrance, 1:11am, was an accident or a coincidence, but more about this special number later.

You did not have to be clairsentient to sense the Presence of

God in this house. Everyone who visited commented on the vibrations of peace and serenity in my home. The former church had been consecrated to God and, like the residence in Philadelphia, possessed a high spiritual aura. I loved living in its special vibration.

I tried to keep my area of the house reminiscent of the time when this house served God as His House. I placed statues of angels, the Virgin Mary, St. Anthony, St. Theresa and Jesus around my flat. Each room had a statue or holy card in every corner. I had a holy card of the Holy Face of Jesus on top of my stove in the kitchen and, for some inexplicable reason, I moved it one afternoon immediately before I was scheduled to give a reading. I don't know what moved me to move the card, but within the hour I regretted my action.

When my client arrived, I seated her at my reading table. She sat facing me and my angels, while I faced her and my open style kitchen. She was stressed out, tearful and suicidal. Long story short, she was at the end of the affair. She had spent ten years involved with a married man and had recently been dumped by him. He had paid all of her expenses for the last decade and now had cut off her cash flow and their relationship. She told me she was totally alone, had no friends, she had dropped them all ten years ago after meeting this man. She believed there was no answer but suicide to end her mounting problems. When I suggested that she turn to her family for support, she informed me that this wasn't possible. She had abandoned her family for this man whom she had made her raison d'etre.

I listened compassionately and did not judge her as she poured her heart out to me. Every type of support group or idea I came up with to help her heal was rejected. She insisted suicide was her only option. As she gave me more reasons why this was her only way out of her dilemma, my eyes were distracted by something going on in my kitchen. I couldn't believe what I was seeing, but it was right in front of my eyes. Three black demons were fighting in my kitchen, swirling in anger in front of the stove where I had removed the holy card of the Holy Face of Jesus.

I counseled the woman, made arrangements for her to get professional help, then walked her to the subway. After I had done this, I stopped at a Catholic church and filled up on holy water. When I returned home, the first thing I did (and I couldn't do it fast enough) was retrieve the Holy Face of Jesus Card, apologizing out loud that I was ever so stupid to have moved Him. Yes, I promised Him that would never happen again. I placed the card back on the stove, sprinkled salt and holy water in every room.

Who talks to holy cards? I do! And if you had seen those three ugly, fighting, frantic, evil spirits I had seen, you would be talking to holy cards too (I was really talking to Jesus asking His forgiveness for my stupidity).

There is a well known psychic, who professes that there is no devil, no Satan. I heartily disagree with her. There is Good and Evil in the universe. There is a battle going on right now. It began when St. Michael threw Satan out of heaven and cast him into the lower astral realms. This battle will continue till Christ comes again. Whenever anyone tells me that there is no Satan or any such thing as demons, I tell them about the demons I saw in my flat.

Which has been my most spirit filled home? It's my childhood home of course, back in Pennsylvania. My parents are in spirit or, if you like, in heaven. But I do believe God allows our loved ones to visit us when we need their help and guidance or for special occasions that we celebrate in our lives.

My sister told me amazing stories about hearing our parents upstairs, the bedsprings squeaked, the toilet flushed on its own. I suggested that she take a long needed vacation!

One year later, while visiting for Christmas, my next door

neighbor, confided to me that every morning at 11am she heard the faucet turn on in our kitchen. She swore she heard my mother next door making her morning cup of tea. The next morning, I had coffee with Violet next door. At exactly 11am, the faucet in my kitchen next door turned on by itself. Someone was definitely in the kitchen with Dinah or, in this case, with Bette. Violet couldn't resist, 'There, see. I told you.' I couldn't argue with her. I had heard it too. I knew no one had my key to the house; it was next to my coffee cup. I had locked the front door and my sister was at work. Did the plumbing have a mind of its own that day? Or was my mom just making herself at home? After this, I was no longer a doubting Thomas and believed my sister and Violet Dudeck.

That New Year's Eve, I decided to stay home and prepare a meal for a New Year's lunch for my neighbors. I set up a buffet table and seating for the guests, prepared the food, and congratulated myself for being ahead of the game. I enjoyed a quiet December 31st at home and thought I was alone until 11 pm when I began to hear a heavenly choir of angels upstairs. Yes, the activity was quite strong that night, with an aura of peace and joy. The singing was beautiful and I considered it a special blessing from God, allowing me to hear what my friends and family in spirit heard every day. I was grateful and feeling honored that God had bestowed a 'bleed through' for me to enjoy the praises that He hears from those who worship Him.

The most phenomenal 'bleed through' that I ever experienced occurred one day in meditation. I suddenly found myself in another lifetime. I was in the Holy Land with a large group of people. We were sitting on a hillside. There were thousands of us there that day. I was very poor in that lifetime, but was rich beyond treasures being there. I heard the most beautiful Voice I had ever heard and will ever hear. The Man speaking was reciting The Beatitudes. It was Jesus. I wanted to stay with Him forever. I never wanted to leave Him. It was perfect bliss. His

Voice exuded His Divine Love with every Word. His Presence was all encompassing Love. There is no other way to describe it. Being in His Presence and hearing His Voice was all I wanted. I needed nothing else. That mystical experience was the epitome of spiritual ecstasy. If that's what eternity will be like, I am ready for His Return. I need no one or nothing else but Him.

Cleansing a House

If your house is home to restless, pesky spirits, who have not yet entered into the Light, there are several things you can do to restore calm and balance to your home. I advise anyone to sprinkle salt at each entrance to their home. Nothing evil can step over salt. Smudging with sage, which I learned from Native Canadians, cleanses your home of negativity.

For a triple cleansing, I smudge sage, sprinkle blessed holy water around each room and have a priest bless my home every January. Sometimes I find it necessary to cleanse my home after someone has visited and left their bad vibes here. Or, if they cried, I open the windows and back door after they leave to let in fresh air, and smudge, sprinkle salt and ring a small bell to rid my home of their sadness. I don't want it staying with me. I never shake hands with anyone. The reason for this is that I do not want any negative black tar built up in someone's aura, to enter mine. This black tar is well known in Energy Healing. It blocks the flow of chi in your body. Energy healers can see this tar, which identifies physical illness in your body. They can remove it with energy healing.

Smudging

Smudging is a sacred ceremony performed to cleanse your home of negative spirits who exist on the lower astral plane. They have not yet crossed over into the Light. They may even be former owners of your home, who don't realize they have died and are going about their daily routine, just as they did when they were on earth in their physical body. When you smudge, you'll be using the spirit of sacred plants to remove negativity, whether from a spirit, or a person who has visited you and deposited their negative energy in your home.

The most commonly used sacred plants used to smudge are sage, cobalt, sweetgrass and cedar. You can also smudge objects. For instance, if someone has given you a gift that just doesn't 'feel right' you can either discard it or pass it through the sacred smoke as you smudge it. Smudge sticks are dried leaves, bound together and rolled into a cylindrical wand. (You can buy them at most metaphysical bookstores, or at your city's native center if there is one where you live. In Toronto, the center is located in The Annex.) Light your smudge bundle. Once it begins to smolder, blow out the flame and proceed to move the stick in a clockwise motion to start cleansing.

Perform this ceremony with an attitude of respect and gratitude to the spirit of the plant. Thank the plant as you finish your smudging ritual. If you are smudging a person, pass the smudge stick around them starting at their feet. Work your way up through their aura, letting the smoke waft around them. When you reach their crown chakra, work the smudge stick down through their aura along their spine. You can smudge as often as you find it necessary, whether for your home, a friend or object, until harmony and balance are restored.

Chapter 3

What is a Reading?

Perhaps you have had a reading, perhaps not. Every mystic, clairvoyant, clairaudient, psychic, has their own style of tuning in and reading your energy. I am a clairvoyant, which means I have visions of the future when I speak with someone. I work on a voice vibration, tuning into the energy in a person's voice. This is why you can receive an accurate reading over the telephone. Spirit works on a voice vibration. Remember, if you go to a reader and decide to give them the silent treatment and won't talk to them because you want to 'test' them, be careful. Your plan may backfire. Many readers work on this voice system and when they don't hear your voice, they simply won't be able to give you any messages.

I am also clairaudient, which means I hear messages from angels, spirit guides, and loved ones who have crossed over to the Higher Side of Life. Being clairsentient, I can sense and feel upcoming events on a personal level, or on a global scale. If you are interested in consulting someone in your area, proceed with due diligence. Stay away from anyone who offers to take a curse off of your life by burning candles for you, after charging you a thousand dollars. Do not fall for this old scam. You can buy two dozen candles at your dollar store and burn them yourself. You'll get better results and you'll have saved $998.00.

Many times I have described events to someone sitting with me for a personal reading. The person will comment, 'That just happened. How did you know that?' When I do a reading, my angel will show visions to me. Some are of the past, some of the present, and others are of the future. At times, someone who has experienced a breakup will come to ask if their ex will return. I might receive a vision of a restaurant where the couple enjoyed a wonderful meal and a night out on the town. When this happens, my angel is telling the person that it happened once and it will happen again. Don't worry, they'll be back.

Of course, the opposite happens where I am shown that the ex was not meant to be their life partner and won't be back. If you ever receive information along those lines from your adviser, don't be upset. God will bring you your right partner at the right time. They will fill your life in ways you have only dreamed of before. And please don't get mad at your reader; it is not their fault.

When there is a good rapport with a person, the visions and messages flow effortlessly. I have been asked if I have ever been unable to read someone. Yes, that has happened. It has happened when I have told someone a series of upcoming events and their response was, 'That will never happen.' Or, they responded, 'No, that can't happen because...' and then they recited twenty reasons why God can not heal or restore their life. Recently, a woman called me, concerned about her autistic nephew. I informed her of the latest treatments for autism which are having good results. This woman began to scream at me that there is no cure for autism and that nothing would ever help her nephew. I wondered what the purpose of her call was. When someone is that closed off to possibility thinking, there is no sense in me continuing to speak to them and wasting my time and energy. God didn't put me on earth to argue. If He had, I'd be a lawyer not a clairvoyant.

Speaking of lawyers, it's only common sense for a seer not to give legal or medical advice. Have I? Yes, I have. In one reading, a client told me she was going to win $250,000.00 in an upcoming lawsuit. I told her, 'No, you won't. You're only going to receive $75,000.00.' I was shown the amount in a vision. I knew she did not like hearing that, but guess who was right? My angel, Francis, was right once more. He's a Messenger of God and his messages are accurate.

Medical Advice

As well as not possessing a law degree, I also do not have the letters MD after my last name. Still, people persist in asking me health questions. I consistently advise them to see their doctor or get a referral to a specialist, but the second opinion they seek is mine. At these times, I remember how St. Pio handled these situations. He was the monk who knew when people would be healed, or if they were going to die. If he saw them recovering, Padre would give the exact date of the healing. If he saw they would not recover, he replied, 'We will let this rest in God's Hands.' I may be given the date the person's healing will occur, or I may receive the name of the doctor or specialist they should book an appointment with for their second opinion. Or I may know of a doctor or hospital setting up clinical trials for a new treatment and refer them. Please, if you are in need of medical advice don't depend on a psychic. See your family doctor and get a referral if you need one.

A Father's Concern

In September, 1989, an East Indian gentleman, the father of twin daughters, came to see me. He had no questions about his marriage, finances or his career. He had just one request. He handed me a photo of his daughters and asked what I picked up with the girls. I was instantly drawn to the daughter on the right. I gabbed for twenty minutes about this little girl. I totally ignored her sibling. I moved forward in time to September 6th. I described the day and what the little girl on the right would be doing. Instantly his face lit up. He revealed to me that she was having heart surgery on September 5th. He had come to me to see if she would live through the surgery. Yes, she would not just survive the surgery, but thrive. Again, I'm not a doctor, but I was allowed to know his daughter would live. A week later, I received a thank you call from him to let me know his daughter had successfully made it through her surgery. It's times like that that humble me. It makes me grateful to God for allowing me to help others. I only know what God allows me to know.

A Daughter's Concern

Around the same time, I received a call from a worried woman. That's nothing new in my line of service. Her worry was for her father who had a heart condition. Her dad was scheduled for a procedure known as an angioplasty. An angioplasty is an operation to repair a damaged blood vessel or unblock a coronary artery. (Once again, I would like to state, if you have a health concern, consult your family physician who can refer you to a medical specialist if need be.) She was calling from Montreal. As I listened to her voice, I felt angioplasty was not necessary for her father. I expressed my feelings to her. As she continued her story, I saw not one but two cardiologists. I relayed my vision to Karen. She replied that this was correct. Her father had been consulting two different doctors at opposite ends of Montreal. As she said that, I saw a crucifix form above one of the doctors, and above the other I saw the Star of David. I felt pulled to follow the advice of the Jewish doctor and advised her accordingly. She laughed merrily and said, 'Dr. Kirsch has told dad he doesn't need angioplasty.' In the end, her father chose Dr. Kirsch. The doctor used alternative therapies instead of angioplasty with positive results.

A Mother's Concern

Another example of medical advice showing up in a reading, but with a twist, happened when a woman came to ask about her children. I'll call her Mrs. R. Her children were all grown and starting families of their own. No matter how old or how successful offspring are, parents never seem to stop worrying about their children.

I tuned in to her two oldest children and then to her youngest daughter. She was in her early thirties and had just given birth to a daughter. The reading was moving along just fine, when suddenly my angel gave me the name Andrew. Never one to doubt my angel (I have learned my lessons), I gave the name Andrew to her. Immediately she informed me, in no uncertain terms, that her daughter was a happily married woman. Her daughter would never have an affair. Her daughter, and husband, Joe (not Andrew), were faithful to each other. An affair was not only out of character, it was totally out of the question.

I assured her that just because I heard the name Andrew, I was not insinuating an affair was on the horizon. Spirit kept reiterating the name Andrew, so I knew it was significant for her. I told her to write the name down and remember it. It was important. Somewhere in the near future, she would meet Andrew and be glad she did. It was one of those moments where I had confused someone. So many times, I have given information to clients, which simply didn't make sense. Should this ever happen to you in a reading, remember the words, because, although the information may make no sense to you at the time of your reading, in time, it will make perfect sense. There is always a reason for you to be given the information. Spirit knows that. In time, you'll understand just like Mrs. R. did.

Ten days later, Mrs. R., called me. A few days after we met, her daughter collapsed and went into a coma. She was rushed by ambulance to the nearest hospital and was admitted to the ER. The family met the neurologist on call that night, Dr. Andrew X. Now, not only did she believe me, she wanted another reading. I told her not to worry, all would be well. Another reading wasn't necessary. I could tell by her voice vibration, coming through the phone, that everything would be fine with her daughter.

I discourage people from getting too many readings. You can become over-read and also become dependent on the reader's advice. This is not a healthy relationship. Co-dependency is not good for you, whether in a personal relationship or otherwise. The mediums who taught me advised that one reading a year is sufficient. You must live your life and not expect answers to come from another person. The Kingdom of God is within. Call on Him. Go into the silence. He's ready to listen and answer you 24/7.

A third example of medical information coming through spontaneously happened July 31, 2001. A close friend, and neighbor, stopped by that evening. He had been diagnosed with Non Hodgkins Lymphoma. He came to say his last goodbye. I hated to disagree with him, but I did. He was not aware that my angel had showed me a vision in 1995. I saw that he would contract this illness and survive. I kept this information to myself. Why upset someone and have them worry unnecessarily for six years? I knew, when the right time arrived, I would step up to the plate. Now was the right time.

I assured my friend that he wasn't going to die. No matter how much I insisted he was going to be fine, he didn't believe me. He thought I was saying it only to make him feel better. Frustrated because he didn't believe me, and upset because the illness had manifested, I silently asked God for help. 'Please God,' I prayed, 'take me into the future so I can convince him his time here on earth isn't up yet.' I closed my eyes and saw his test results for October 4th. He would be in remission then. Thank You, God. I had a vision of Jesus, Who said, 'All he needs is one drop of My Blood,' and with that I accepted that one drop of the Precious Blood would lead to my friend's healing. My friend's reaction was the same one I have received many times. It was complete silence. He may have doubted me, but I did not doubt God that night. Of course, God was right. He always is. On October 4th, my friend received the wonderful news that he was in remission. Dr. Jesus rocks.

Memorable Readings

Early one hot July morning, my telephone rang at 10am. It was a Saturday and I had slept in for once. My first thought was, who in the world is calling me this early? My friends know that I am a night owl, not a morning lark. I hadn't even had a cup of coffee yet. I answered to hear my old friend, Dr. Jake, ringing in from Montreal. He quickly explained that his car had been stolen. Jake wanted to know exactly when the Montreal police would find his car. Firstly, I needed to put the Maxwell House on.

People who request an early morning reading will be greatly disappointed because, in my opinion, I read best after noon. Jake waited patiently. Luckily, this was one time that my angel gave a specific date (this doesn't happen with every reading). I told Jake the car would be found on August 15th. I could hear the disappointment in his voice. I knew he wanted his car back in July but I knew that wasn't going to happen. Spirit added additional information that a valuable item would be recovered from the glove compartment. Jake assured me that he didn't leave anything of value in the glove compartment; he just wanted his car back. My angel begged to differ but I wasn't going to persist. Time would tell. And it did.

In early August, Jake invited me and a few other friends to his chalet in Ellicottville, New York. The topic of his lost car came up during the trip. I reminded Jake that D-Day wasn't until August 15th. His car was going to show up but not before then. There was still time for the car to be found. Secretly, quietly, I was talking to Francis, saying, 'This better not be the first time you're wrong.' Just like first grade, I would be so embarrassed. I had a strong faith, however, and, just like Tug McGraw, I had to believe. I wished that Jake had that same faith in me and my forecast but he was very doubtful that he would ever see his car again. We had fun at the chalet and took a side trip to Lily Dale, in Cassadaiga, New York.

In September, Jake called to get together for lunch. He had

happy news to report. His car had been found in Montreal. He wanted me to know that his new camera was found intact in the glove compartment. Francis was right again. I wondered if Francis was also right about the date the police found his car. He was – It was August 15th. I gently reminded Jake that Francis was, once more, bang on. Go Francis! Go Francis!

I have learned as a clairvoyant that I can't satisfy everyone. The best I can do is to tell the truth.

Another memorable reading was with a Toronto woman, who booked a reading in May of 1989. At the time, I was reading at a bookstore located on Danforth Avenue.

She got right to the point as she settled in for her reading. Her husband worked for a company that decided to transfer him to Vancouver, British Columbia. He recently visited Vancouver and bought a house there. Their Toronto residence was on the market but wasn't moving. They had no browsers let alone buyers and they were anxious to sell their Toronto house. Two mortgages was one too many. Their daughters, however, were rebelling against the move; they had no desire to leave Toronto. They yearned to stay in their childhood home and remain at their high school. Moving meant they would be leaving friends they had known since first grade, and they were not the least bit interested in Vancouver.

I turned on the tape recorder and started the reading.

During the session, I gave her names of people who would be significant to her, including the name Michael. I was hearing these names from my angel. The only name she recognized was her husband's. She became a bit argumentative, stating that the names were meaningless. Here we go again! I received instructions from my angel and I gave them to her. I told her to play the tape back in thirty days. At that time, she would know everyone I had named on it.

To make matters worse, I suddenly had a vision. There was no sense stalling; the reading had to continue. I told her that she would not be moving to Vancouver. Oh boy! If looks could kill, I'd have been six feet under and pushing up daisies.

Why stop now? Francis was on a roll. I continued with the reading. Her daughters would be celebrating because the family would be staying in Toronto. Why mince words? You and your family will remain in Toronto. You are not moving anywhere, I advised her. The girls will be in the same school next year, attend their prom and graduate with their friends in Toronto. Now I knew how the Yankees felt when they were booed at Fenway Park. The atmosphere in my office was somber. You could sense the anger aimed at me in the air. My visions went over like a mink coat sale at a PETA Fundraiser. She wasn't buying any of it.

If this wasn't the reading from hell, it was the one from the 9th Circle of Purgatory. I had talked non-stop for forty-five minutes. She was as expressionless as a mummy, except when she wanted to argue. She broke the silence by asking me, why I was telling her this? I meekly said, 'Don't be mad at me. I'm not making this up. I'm telling you what I am hearing.' She demanded to know where I was getting this information from. Who was telling me this nonsense? I told her I heard it from my Guardian Angel Francis. I pointed to Francis, who was on my right side. I continued, 'I know you can't see him. I can see, and hear him, and he's telling me you're not moving.'

This reading was turning into the nightmare on Danforth Avenue. She heard the worst possible scenario she could ever imagine. Here I was, insisting it was going to transpire, exactly as I said. This reading couldn't end soon enough for my liking or hers.

She wasn't the first person to become argumentative and question my accuracy and she wouldn't be the last.

Ordinarily, my clients thanked me after their readings. I knew not to expect a thank you from her. I breathed a sigh of relief when she finally left my office. I silently thanked God that the reading was over. I never wanted to see her again.

Late in August, Ed the bookstore owner called me in to do a few readings on a Saturday. When I got to work that day, my first client had already arrived. I recognized her immediately and cringed. It was Madame Mummy from May. She was now smiling and relaxed. What in the world can she want? I thought. I soon found out. She reached into her purse and brought out the tape we had recorded back in May. She told me she played the tape after one month, as I had told her to do, and every name on the tape made sense. She knew, in thirty days, everyone my angel had said she would know.

Over time, it all materialized. There's that word again – time. If only we understood the true nature of it and didn't automatically panic when we don't receive what we want exactly at the moment we want it. We need to learn to trust God to work our situations out in His way, in His time, according to His perfect plan.

She informed me that the family was staying in Toronto. Her husband's employer had cancelled his move to Vancouver. Her daughters were thrilled. Now her only question was when her house in Vancouver was going to sell. As Yogi Berra said, 'It's déjà vu all over again.'

More Memorable Readings

1989 was anything but a dull year. Another reading I'll never forget was a young lady from the West End. She began her reading by handing me a picture of her boyfriend, George. George was a very handsome man. As I held his photo, I saw dark visions and heard my angel say, 'Tell her to run five hundred miles in the opposite direction from George.'

I told her exactly what Francis had said to me. She told me she was deeply in love with George. She hoped to marry him. The more she gushed about George and how she wanted to marry him, the more my angel disagreed with her plan. Francis then got right to the point and told me what this man's profession was. He was an enforcer, and not for the Toronto Parking Authority. When I confronted her with this point she came clean and admitted it was true. You can't conceal the truth from an angel, especially my Francis. The next day, I received a visit at work from two gentlemen from an agency that specialized in curtailing organized crime activities. They asked for me by my full name. No one knew my last name. My boss never gave out his employee's last names but I discovered that he had broken this rule the day before when Ms. Moll requested my last name. I found out later that this woman had been on her phone gossiping about the accuracy of her reading with me. Apparently, her phone-line had been tapped and that is how the detectives knew where to find me.

Another unforgettable reading that summer was with a client from Oakville, Ontario. This young lady was in love with Robert. As she said his name, I got the sensation of my nasal passages dripping down the back of my throat. This is how spirit tells me someone is using cocaine. He wasn't just using it; he was dealing it and pimping as his second career. She had come to me for a reading, not a morality lecture. I did not ridicule her choice of marriage material. I went into the future for her and revealed what I saw coming into her life.

I told her that Robert would become close friends with her father. Her reaction to this prediction was that I was totally wrong. Her father could not stand Robert. In fact, she used the H word, a word I avoid using at all costs. I don't want to draw the negative power and chaos attached to it into my life. Her father hated Robert. She stated vehemently that the two of them would never, could never, be friends. I told her that I was moving forward in time, and by August she would see their friendship come to pass. Then, I had a vision of her birthday. My goodness, I was seeing her breaking up with Robert over dinner. This vision surprised me; it was going to shock her, I thought. I continued, 'On your birthday, you and Robert will go out to dinner and you are going to be the one who breaks off the relationship.' She burst into tears at those words. My predictions have often been met with this reaction.

She vehemently insisted that she loved this man, wanted to marry him and have a family together. I silently thought, you have got to be kidding me. I envisioned my mother reading me the riot act if it was me in her situation. I had to remember that it wasn't for me to judge her and Robert, but to help her. In forty-five minutes, I was done going forward in time, prophesying and predicting. Her reading was over. She only had one last thing to say to me. It was, 'Betsy, you have me so upset right now, I want to go home and commit suicide.' I wondered how many seers have ever had that said to them, or was I the only one? I knew suicide was not going to stop her pain.

Compassion kicked in as I wrote my home telephone number on a piece of paper. I told her to call me before she went through with any suicide plan. I would give her a free reading at my home. She left my office with a handful of tissues and my phone number. I believed in the accuracy of the reading and knew without a doubt that Robert would be out of her life on her birthday, which was September 4th.

Once more, I hadn't told her what she wanted to hear. I told the bitter truth. At the time of the reading, it was bitter for her to hear it but I knew God always made something good out of the worst of times. I expected to receive a phone call from her within the week, but I didn't.

The Rolling Stones were playing in Toronto on Labor Day, September 4th, that year. My boyfriend and I had tickets. I couldn't wait to see Mick and the boys. We were all set to go, when my phone rang. It was Ms. Oakville. It was her birthday. She wanted to see me. She had to see me. Oh boy! Why this and why now? But I was the one who had told her to call me if she needed me and I had said I would give her a free reading at my home and I had to keep my word. I called my boyfriend and told him that I had an emergency and couldn't make the concert. I couldn't believe I gave up a Stones concert to counsel someone who would be crying at my kitchen table in less than an hour. That wasn't the way I had planned to spend the last long weekend of the summer. But someone was depending on me to be there for them. It was time for me to do the right thing.

When she arrived, I couldn't believe it was the same person I had read in June. That girl was co-dependent, weak, sad, depressed, hopeless and suicidal. The girl at my kitchen table was beaming. She was happy, laughing, cheerful, joyful, glowing. There were no tears. What had happened? Now, it was me who was in shock. All of Francis's crazy predictions had come true, that's what had happened. She was thankful they had. That made two of us. She updated me with the latest news. Yes, her dad had become very close with Robert. They became so close that her father took Robert to his private country club where they played golf together every weekend. It didn't get more surprising than this. Was I hearing this right? Now, her father loved Robert. Had I heard her say the word love instead of hate? I had. I have received a few psychic reading update shockers in my life but this jolt was about to top my list for the year.

She told me that Robert was taking her out later that night for dinner. It was her birthday and he wanted to make it a special night. She had a special plan of her own. She planned to dump Robert at the restaurant. Now I was super stunned but so happy for her. She went from being a needy, clingy, insecure, victim, to a self-confident, self-assured, empowered woman, whose spiritual eyes had been opened. We have our physical eyes and then we have our spiritual eyes. When we see with our spiritual eyes, we are in touch with God. He reveals truths to us and stops our suffering. My client from Oakville was living proof of this. It's times like these that I thank God once more, for allowing me to help people and letting me work with my wonderful angel

Francis. Out of utter despair, God can create great joy. Yes, the most memorable people have been those that are either skeptics or can't possibly believe that events will transpire as I have told them they will. In the end, it's wonderful to share in their joy and happiness.

A happy post-script to this story occurred in 2003. The Rolling Stones have had a love affair with Toronto that goes back decades when they first gave a surprise concert at The El Macambo in the 1970's with special guest, Margaret Trudeau. When SARS struck the city in 2003, they came to the rescue to revive our suffering economy by performing a benefit concert. The Rolling Stones helped to restore tourism around the GTA. Everyone speculated where the band would practice before the concert. The Elmo was a good guess and an inaccurate one. A new private school, the Greenwood College School, had opened in Toronto on Mt. Pleasant Road. The school, around the corner from my home, turned out to be the venue where The Stones practiced at night. The headmaster at Prince Andrew's alma mater happened to be one of the co-founders of GCS, which might have influenced their choice. Some friends and I happened to be allowed in one evening, on the spur of the moment, to listen to them rehearse. My karma returned to me fourteen years later in spectacular fashion. And the concert was unforgettable too.

The most touching and meaningful stories involve bringing children, who have crossed over, through to their parents. One evening, I answered my phone to hear a woman on the other end say, 'I hope you can help me.' She was crying. Through her tears she explained that her oldest son had died. She was having a rough time coping since his funeral. I told her that I would try my best to make the connection for her with her son.

Her son came through instantly, describing the details of the night he had died in a car accident. He told me what his mother was doing the night his best friend came to her house with the news of his fatal accident. The connection, the bond of love, between mother and son was as strong as ever. It had not been broken. This made it easier to convey his messages. He described several family events which he had recently attended. His mother confirmed these events. Then, I was shown a vision of his mother standing in his bedroom, admiring his gold medal. I couldn't think of an Olympic athlete who had been killed in a car accident in the past year. Surely, I would have remembered his name. I was apprehensive about relaying this message as I did not want to cause his mother increased pain. But I had been taught to give the messages that I get from spirit and trust, so I related this vision to her. She confirmed that her son had won a gold medal in track, in the Special Olympics. She was crying stronger than when I had first picked up the receiver, and tears welled up in my eyes too. It was the most humbling experience, and I will never forget it. Our conversation came to an end as she thanked me for helping her. The honor – the privilege – was mine. I thanked God that I was available to speak with this wonderful mother and her son.

I have a close friend whose daughter crossed over to the Other Side of Life in 1999. Our paths intersected July 9, 2008. My friends marvel at my photographic memory and ability to remember the exact day when we met. When I meet someone for the first time, and know we will be friends for life, I have no problem remembering details of our initial meeting. I know that every person I have met came into my life for a reason, even if they are in my life for only a few weeks, months, or years. Then, there are those who have so much in common with me, I know that we were destined to meet and will remain lifelong friends. That's the way I felt the evening I met my friend, whom I will call Marie.

Before Marie arrived, I tuned into her daughter and asked what she would like me to tell her mother. Often times, loved ones will visit me prior to their family member's appointment to tell me what to focus on. They will tell me what the most important questions are to answer and what their relative should do about certain situations. Our family and friends in the next dimension really do care about what is going on in our lives and they want the best for us, just like God cares and wants the best for us.

Some messages came through for Marie. I jotted them down so I wouldn't forget them. Marie arrived promptly at six. Her daughter came through immediately with messages. The first message was in reference to her mother's business. Next, a more personal message came through. Marie's daughter wanted her mother to know that when Marie had breakfast, and buttered her toast with the special pate knives, she was with her. Marie burst into tears. My new friend told me that when her daughter was alive on earth, attending school, they never had breakfast together because their schedules were not in synch. Her daughter wanted to reassure Marie that now they were having breakfast together every day. Her daughter described the kitchen area to me and wanted her mother to know that she is there with her every morning.

Before we knew it, it was 9 pm. Did I feel drained? No, I wasn't drained; I was energized. Love is energy. That evening with Marie and her daughter, my home was filled with love.

Chapter 4

God Has Three Answers: Yes, No and Not Tonight

For over thirty years, I have told people that God has three answers. They are: yes, no and not tonight. You should see the reaction when during a reading someone suddenly realizes that their answer is not tonight. We live in the instant society; we enjoy instant coffee, instant soup, microwave meals; pizza is delivered in thirty minutes or it's free. Who wants to wait? We don't like to wait for a bus, for a job, for a house, or for love. We don't like to wait for anything or anyone.

From Here to Eternity

I will never forget one woman who wanted to know when her boyfriend would return. As we spoke, I had a vision of the calendar. Spirit showed me the 31st of the month. I told her that he would be back at the end of the month. She had three weeks to wait. When she realized I did not say, 'He will call you tonight,' she lost her temper. She proceeded to tell me that she couldn't possibly wait three weeks – that was too long. If he didn't call her that night, she would commit suicide. I asked her if she had any concept of the amount of time eternity represented. She told me that she did. I advised her to consider the three weeks for her ex to call her compared to waiting from here through eternity for him to get back in touch. I made my point; she got it. Yes, her boyfriend did come back in three weeks and they have been happily married for twenty years. The next time you become impatient, put your situation in perspective. When you pray and don't receive an immediate answer, don't become discouraged. There is a reason why your answer is not tonight.

Pray without ceasing and anticipate your answer with hope.

Teaching Patience to an Impatient World

We just can't wait. Children anxiously wait for Christmas. A bewildered female waits and wonders if and when her ex-boyfriend will return. The tired job-seeker waits for that phone call to come and tell them they aced that interview and can start next week. Authors wait for the launch of a long-awaited book. Perhaps we need to take another look at the way we see this waiting period. I have come to realize that this waiting time is actually a gift given to us to prepare for the best. It may also be time for us to do some work on ourselves and the manuscripts of our lives.

If there is a separation period in your relationship, God is not punishing you. It may be that both of you need to grow, or grow up. None of us are finished growing and learning as long as we are breathing. There is always room for each of us to grow and improve. If you find yourself in this situation, use this time to pray, meditate and ask for guidance. Ask how you can contribute to the relationship to balance it. But don't think that it is your sole responsibility to fix the relationship. Pray for your partner that their spiritual eyes are opened and they realize what their contribution should be. Make time for yourself. Don't sit around waiting for your other half to show up. There were two people in the relationship. Value yourself. Treat yourself the way you deserve and want to be treated. Take yourself out to dinner and a movie. Treat yourself to something you have wanted to do for some time but postponed. Perhaps it's a night at the museum or a gallery opening. Now is the time. Don't wait to treat yourself well. Begin to do it now.

This applies also if you are between jobs. Yes, it is a job searching for a job. Don't isolate yourself. That's the worst thing you can do at the time you need support the most. Stay connected to family and friends. Don't withdraw. Speak in a positive manner. Words are powerful and what you say out loud will manifest, so be sure to state how the right job/position/career is looking for you, just as much as you are looking for it and you expect it to arrive soon. You'll be amazed at the positive results you receive from this simple exercise. There is more help for you in the affirmations section in chapter ten.

Spirit Doesn't Know Time

When people ask a medium or clairvoyant for a specific time, they will hear what every seer knows, 'Spirit doesn't know time'. God is outside of time. That is not just an escape hatch for the reader. Don't ask me to explain Quantum Physics, but Einstein said that there is no time or space and this has proven itself to be the case. Before I give an example of spirit not knowing time, I will share a story of when spirit knew the exact date:

A divorced woman could not get over her ex-husband. No matter how hard I tried to explain to her that her marriage of twenty-five years was over, she would not take no for her answer. She insisted that she was a devout Irish Catholic and never wanted the divorce in the first place. She demanded to know when she would see her husband again. Trusting in God, and Francis, I gave her the date I was told – September 7th. She wanted more details. She wanted the date they would remarry, but I did not see that happening. All I was told by Francis was the date that she would see her ex. No date for a remarriage was given.

L. called me at home almost every evening after that to make sure that September 7th was the correct date. I assured her that she would see her ex-husband on that day. Francis had said it loud and clear, make no mistake about it. Although I included in each conversation that I did not see a remarriage with her ex, she continued to be in denial about that point. Her former husband called her in mid-August and requested to see her. He suggested they meet on September 7th. I received a call from L. proclaiming me the greatest medium since Doris Collins. I wasn't the least bit surprised that the date was correct but I still did not hear wedding bells ringing for those two.

On the night of September 7th, my phone rang after 10 pm. It was a distraught L. she was more upset than ever. Yes, she had met her ex at the assigned time and location, but she hadn't expected to be introduced to his new bride to be, whom he had brought along to their meeting. Finally, Lorna had to admit the truth and accept it. I was never shown the new bride in the reading, but I had been told that L.'s ex had moved on and she was not going to be moving on with him. The time had come for her to move on in another direction. A move to Vancouver had come up in her reading and within a year it materialized for her.

Accident Warning

My friend, Helen Main, who was a medium at the Britten Memorial Spiritualist Church, had warned her nephew to be careful when riding his bike. She had a vision of him being struck by a car and breaking his right leg. She cautioned him to be especially careful during the month of September. September came and went with no accident. Her nephew chided Helen and told her she was not such a great clairvoyant. In September the next year, Helen's nephew was hit by a car while riding his bike and suffered a broken right leg just as she had foretold. Spirit may not reveal the precise month, day and year to you in a reading, but spirit never lies. In a reading, it may be the way your clairvoyant or seer interprets the timeframe they receive. Keep that in mind if things don't materialize for you exactly when you think they will.

I was told of future events in my life by two well known clairvoyants, Valerie Morrison and John Deere. Both told me years ago that I would be interviewed on television and radio. I filed their predictions away, thinking they had confused me with a friend who was a radio host at WMGK in Philadelphia. Their forecasts came true in ways I never expected. In these instances, spirit went more than fifteen years into the future. It takes time for your life to unfold, so be patient.

Have you ever told God when He should answer your prayers? And how He should answer them? When He didn't answer them when or how you wanted them answered, did you become frustrated or mad at God? You gauge your life by clocks and calendars, but God is outside of time, and answers you at the best time – His appointed time. God is never late.

Five Years for a Business Turnaround

In 1992, a businessman from Montreal requested a reading. He wanted to know when business would turn around. I wanted to tell him in two weeks, but in his reading I saw it would take five years for his business to bounce back and be profitable. There was light at the end of the tunnel. There always is. In the meantime, I had great news; my angel showed me visions of him signing a contract with one of the top modeling agencies in Canada. He would not just model but he would also be chosen for television commercials. I saw him traveling to the United States and moving to Miami, Florida. I was so happy for him. He was less than thrilled. He told me, in no uncertain terms, that he had no desire whatsoever to be a model. Being cast in commercials was even less interesting to him. I have had people react sadly to some of my predictions but I had never seen such disappointment as his. This client was also a friend and did not speak to me for five years. His silence was deafening and hurt me deeply.

Five years passed. During the holidays it's a natural tendency to look back and reminisce about old friends and the good times shared together, and on December 20th, 1997, I sensed that my Montreal friend, whom I will call Jean, was very close. Although we hadn't seen each other or spoken to each other in five years,

I just knew he had been thinking of me. Within twenty minutes, my phone rang. It was our mutual friend, Dr. Jake. He called to say that Jean was in from Miami, Florida. He proceeded to tell me that all of my predictions for Jean, from 1992, had come true. Jean wanted to schedule a reading with me but was afraid to call me. He thought I was mad because I had been ignored for so long, and that I most likely held a grudge. Grudges are for people who live on a low vibration. Jake was calling to give me Jean's number.

The ball was in my court. As soon as we hung up, I called Jean and arranged to see him later that week. It was great to reconnect after so many years. It was even greater to hear his exciting stories of working with the Ford Modeling Agency and flying to New Orleans to shoot a commercial. As I have said before, spirit never lies. If you have a reading and you're not pleased with what you've been told, remember my friend Jean. At the time of his reading, he could not have curbed his enthusiasm more. With the passage of time, he did see things from a different perspective and it all worked out in his favor for his highest good. Now go call a friend you haven't spoken to in a long time. I'm sure they'll be happy to hear from you. It will make their day and yours too. If you have been holding a grudge, let go of it. Let go of resentment and rise to a higher vibration.

Spirit Speaks in Symbols

There have been times when I have received specific dates for people in a reading. I see the calendar with a date circled or see a cake lit with candles representing a birthday. Spirit will show me the year and sometimes the day and the month. That means the person will receive their answer when they, a friend or family member, celebrate the birthday I have been shown.

At other times, I might see a home being renovated. I will see a particular room, maybe the kitchen, being remodeled. When that happens, it means the person will receive their answer when the kitchen is finished. It may not be their kitchen being remodeled; it may be their brother or sister who is having the work done, but spirit is very clear when I relay these types of timeframes. The client completely understands what spirit is talking about.

There is an old saying that a girl eventually turns into her mother. I joke with my friends and say, 'I am turning into my dad.' My dad served on a destroyer during WWII and was an avid fisherman throughout his life. What sailor or fisherman doesn't watch the skies and listen incessantly to weather reports? My pop was no exception. I used to tease my dad and tell him if he needed to know the weather just look out the window or to go open the front door and stick his head outside and he would know the weather.

The tables have turned. Now I can't leave home without first checking two different weather shows. In my readings, I receive answers that are weather related. When this happens, I know it is my dad coming through to help out with the timing. When someone is pressing me for a sign of when one of my predictions will come to pass, I receive visions of weather patterns from my dad. I would never wish for disaster or destruction, but I will see a hurricane or a tornado touch down on a state and know that this means the person will receive their answer when that storm or tornado hits.

Can we do anything to make predictions happen faster? Many times I have been asked this question. The answer is no. Let God work it out in His time, in His divine way. Trust Him. When you try to make something happen, you can be guaranteed of only one thing – disappointment. Just like L. kept insisting that she was remarrying her ex, instead she received a bigger disappointment. Never try to force your will upon another person. When you are tempted to manipulate someone, stop. It is time to let go and let God. Put it in His Hands, trust and believe in Him and His Word.

Several years ago someone wanted to know when her newly reconnected relationship would be back to normal. By normal, she meant when she would be seeing Mr. Wonderful three times a week, instead of just once a week. That was a fair question. I totally understood wanting that comfortable feeling of all being well in Loveland. Did spirit give me the exact date when her relationship would be rock solid? No. Spirit showed me a symbol for her to watch for, which represented the time when her relationship would be back to the way she was wishing it to be. I saw a kiwi. The key was in interpreting exactly what this kiwi meant. I knew it was significant and somehow represented when her relationship would be exactly where she wished it to be. Spirit did not spell it out explicitly for me. It was up to me to interpret this symbol. It could appear in a hundred different ways. I gave an example to S.; perhaps she would be at a friend's home and be served kiwi for dessert. I gave her strict orders not to go out and buy a bag of kiwis that night in order to make her prediction come true. The kiwi would show up when it was supposed to without any help from S. or me.

You cannot force your future. Let it unfold naturally. Whenever I receive symbolic messages like this, I tell the person not to try and force it. We cannot force events to happen. We must have patience and let God be God. God's delays are not His denials. That weekend, her boyfriend took her for dinner. He had made the reservation, as he usually did since he lives in downtown Toronto and S. is in the 905 (suburbs). After arriving at the restaurant, they enjoyed a drink in the lounge area. When their waitress seated them in the dining room she placed menus on the table. The restaurant her boyfriend had chosen was The Kiwi Restaurant. S. told me later she got chills when she saw the menu. Symbols don't get more specific than that. Spirit doesn't lie. This marked the turning point in their relationship.

The old comfortable stability returned and S. had a new

question for me; when would she become engaged? I told her I would do my best, but I couldn't guarantee I would be able to tune in to her exact engagement date. I was still recuperating from the kiwi episode. Immediately, I saw a large red heart, a diamond ring and the date February 14th above her head. Valentine's Day, would be the day she would receive her marriage proposal. Spirit was giving the exact day. It was early January, not too long to wait we thought. Valentine's Day came and went that year with no diamond ring for S. She, like Jean, stopped calling me after that, and our friendship was put on ice faster than champagne at the Oscars after-parties. That happens often when my usefulness ends and delays appear in the manifestation of my predictions.

A year passed with no contact from S. I extended an olive branch the next Easter to share some happy news with her. (I will never endorse carrying a grudge). As soon as she heard my voice, she couldn't wait to share her exciting news. She had become engaged on Valentine's Day during a romantic dinner. I was so glad she had taken notes during her conversation with me the prior year. I asked her to go back and find the prediction, when spirit told her she would receive her diamond ring on February 14th. Yes, once again, my angel was correct, but the exact time was 365 days and a few weeks into the future. It was not a month away as S. had hoped but, once more, spirit had not lied.

Symbols Around You

What symbols show up in your life? What do they represent to you? The other day, a friend came by to visit wearing the most beautiful silver necklace with a stunning key on it. I commented how Native Americans wear silver, because it is the purest ore and draws spirit closer to you. Whenever I see someone wearing silver jewelry I mention this. Nine times out of ten they are very much into meditation and their spiritual development. My friend commented that she had had the necklace for years, but never wore it until that day. I told her that keys represent a new beginning, whether in career or relationships, but most of all they foretell of moving your residence. She confided to me that her marriage was over, and that she would be changing residences in the near future. She didn't need to say a word; her jewelry told me everything.

Watch the symbols that appear in your life and you will learn more about what is coming your way. Here are meanings of symbols that might be appearing in your life:

Animals: Watch the animals that appear in your dreams; these can be your totem animals contacting you. Each animal has distinctive traits that relate to your nature. Each animal has its own medicine.

Butterflies: Butterflies represent hope and good luck. Anytime a butterfly comes near me, I think of my friend, June, who collected butterfly pins, pictures and sculptures. To me it is a sign that she is saying hello.

Birds: Making a wish when you see the first robin in spring is an old tradition.

The raven is portrayed as a trickster by Native Americans. Crows are often seen as a bad omen. There were several crows that used to wake me up with their screeching at 5 am every morning. It irritated me to be awoken so early. I used to yell, 'Shut up!' and wished they'd all disappear. Shortly after, West Nile Virus hit and all the crows in my neighborhood really did disappear. Then I wished them back. Be careful what you wish for, you might just get it. Now when I hear a crow cawing I am grateful and bless it and ask forgiveness for my past stupidity.

Stones: Do you find stones appearing as if out of nowhere? Stones and crystals have different properties. I had a friend who kept finding small amber pebbles in her house. She was mystified by these appearances but I wasn't surprised when she became a holistic healer within five years because amber is a healing gem.

Jewelry: I often receive messages from spirit relatives asking their daughters, granddaughters or nieces to please wear the ring, necklace or bracelet they inherited. If you have received such an item from a relative who has crossed over, please start to wear it. So often, I hear spirit wish the jewelry would be worn, not just sit idle in a box. You may find a piece of jewelry outside of your jewelry box. When this happens, it is a sign that your relative or friend in spirit wants you to wear it.

Books: Are books talking to you? Do you find just the right book at the right time? If a book falls out of your bookcase, it is a sign of someone in spirit trying to get your attention. They may have bought the book for you or there is a connection between the book's subject and your friend in spirit.

Money: Finding dimes or quarters in your home, when you know that you definitely did not drop any change, is a message from spirit loved ones on the Other Side. Spirit drops the coins to get your attention and make their presence known to you.

What about numbers? Are there certain numbers that have followed you throughout your life? Think back and see what you were experiencing when certain numbers appeared in your life. The number 116 shows up a lot for me. That was the address of my childhood home, where I lived from age five to ten. It was a very happy period in my life but, more importantly, spirit was communicating with me very strongly at this time in my life. I could sense and see the spirit of the former owner of 116 South Franklin Street. It is also the house where my grandfather first appeared to me after his crossing. It shows up in my life very strongly now. I take it as a good sign, as a message from friends and family on the Other Side of Life who remember those happy times too.

One of my friends told me recently that he keeps seeing 1183 everywhere. I asked him if he realized that when the 8 and 3 are added together, 1111 is following him. We took that as a very good omen for him because 11 and 22 are the highest spiritual numbers. He is going through a major transition now and embraced 1183 as a sign that he is making the right decisions. You may receive confirmation through symbols and numbers but also through very obvious coincidences.

Chapter 5

Intuition

Intuition is an inner knowing. It is that small still voice inside of us. Sometimes we listen to that inner voice, sometimes we ignore it. How often have you felt guided to do something, ignored your gut feeling, only to regret it later? Don't doubt yourself or your intuition. There are documented cases of passengers, who felt compelled to change their cruise on the Titanic to another ocean liner because of their intuition. Your intuition can urge you to change your plans, postpone your plans, or abandon them completely. Never second guess yourself. Learn to trust yourself and your intuition.

Jeane Dixon's Prediction – Intuition/Destiny

Back in the early 1970s, Central Pennsylvania was all abuzz that the Washington D.C. seer, Jeane Dixon, had made a prediction on a national television talk show that the Harrisburg East Mall would be hit with an explosion before Christmas. The mall was my favorite shopping center. I assured my parents that I would not be holiday shopping there that December. I have never been one to press my luck or tempt fate. Pomeroy's in downtown Harrisburg would do just fine for my presents.

One evening in mid-December, a friend came by to help me decorate my Christmas tree. The tree looked festive, but had obvious bare spots. It needed a few more decorations to fill the gaps. Charles and I still had time to buy decorations before the stores closed. We headed out into the frosty night in my car, in the opposite direction of the East Mall. I made it absolutely clear to my friend that we were not going to the East Mall because of Jeane Dixon's prediction. I didn't care if he thought I was nuts.

She was known to be accurate, so we were taking no chances. In fifteen minutes, we arrived at W.T. Grants. We entered close to 9 pm, so we needed to snap it up and shop in a hurry. I found decorations and hurried to the check-out counter with Charles in tow. We were the last customers to exit the store that night. Returning home, we hung the last few decorations and tossed the tinsel on the tree.

The next morning, I turned on the local news before heading out to work at the Pennsylvania Department of Justice. The lead story was a gas explosion, which had occurred the night before, shortly after 9 pm, at the W.T. Grants store – the store where my friend and I had done our last minute shopping. I immediately rang Charles and told him how lucky we had been. The lesson I learned that day was that no matter how I had tried to avoid disaster, I went walking right towards it. I have come close many times, but my number wasn't up that night. My intuition did not guide me away from the explosion but it wasn't my destiny to die that night either.

Best Friend Ignored Her Intuition

I wish my best friend had followed her intuition. It was the Thursday before her upcoming wedding, and she confided to me that she had doubts about marrying her husband to be. Sensing the disappointment in her voice, I told her that she still had time to call the whole thing off and cancel the nuptials. No, she wasn't about to take my advice. Why? Because the church and hall were booked months ago and the invitations had been sent and returned. Everything was a go for Saturday. My power of persuasion was zero. The wedding went off as scheduled, and she lived to regret it. She regretted it to the day her husband not only physically attacked her, but put a gun to her head and threatened to end her life. If only she had listened to what her intuition had told her.

Seven years later, I was reminded again of how important it

is to be true to yourself and follow your intuition. My friend, Helen, was giving messages at church, and gave one to a young woman in the congregation. Spirit was well aware that she was engaged and going to be married by the end of the month. The message was direct and straight to the truth. 'You know the marriage is going to fail. You are marrying the wrong person, and you know it. Call it off.' At those words, the woman burst into tears and admitted it was true. She knew she was with the wrong man but the invitations had been sent and the church and hall had been booked last year. I had the old déjà vu all over again feeling. If you ever receive a similar message from a medium, listen to them, and avoid the upcoming pain. You will thank God you did.

The National Domestic Violence Hotline in the U.S.A. is 1-800-799-SAFE (7233). The Canadian Clearing House on Family Violence is 1-800-267-1291.

Intuition Saved Me/Mother's Intuition

My intuition saved my life the night before I moved to Miami, Florida. To say goodbye to my hometown, Shamokin, I decided one last drive through town was apropos to bid farewell. It was a quiet summer night, not much going on in the middle of the week. I headed home just before 11pm but noticed someone was following me. I wondered if it was one of my friends who had spotted me on Independence Street. There was no way this was going to turn into a late night gab fest. I had a train to catch at the 30th Street Station in Philadelphia the next morning and I wasn't going to miss it. Sure enough, as I parked my Mustang in front of our house, I recognized someone who had attended my high school. He asked me to hop in his car and go for a ride. I explained that I was moving to Florida the next day and couldn't possibly stay out late. I glanced over at the front door and there was my mother standing waiting for me. She never did that. My parents always left the porch light on but no one ever stood at the front door waiting for me. I told R. I'd see him next summer when I would be home on vacation. As I met my mom at the door, I asked her why she had stood there waiting for me. She said she just had a feeling – call it Mother's Intuition. I told her that R. had asked me to go for a ride with him, but I had made a rain-check to meet up with him next summer. We didn't think any more of it that night. The next day, I was off to Miami.

A year later, I was an even bigger believer in Mother's Intuition when Mom's weekly letter arrived in my mailbox, in Coconut Grove. It was the fall of the year and she had enclosed a newspaper clipping from the *Shamokin News Item*. It was the story of three young girls who had been murdered the previous summer. They had been murdered the night I had been followed home by R. He was now one of three males being held on murder charges. I immediately dialed long distance and blurted out, 'Mom, do you realize? Had I accepted the offer to go for a ride that night, I might have been one of these girls.' We recalled how she, uncharacteristically, had waited at the front door for me. My mom never went to bed until I came home, but that night she told me she just had to go and wait at the door for me. Her Mother's Intuition was in high gear.

Not every episode of intuition is as dramatic as this one. When I reflect on that night, I realize that if I had not been moving the next day, I might very well have accepted R.'s invitation.

Intuition Merging with Dreams

There have been times when a dream and my intuition have merged. In dreamland one night, I found myself driving a black Mercedes. It was one of those lucid dreams that seem so real that you know it is more than just a dream. It's a message for you to remember. Upon waking, I thought, that was nice, but I am not in the market for a new car. I was in the market for a new residence because, once more, my landlord was selling his house that my friends and I were renting, but not a car.

If you're like me, you are very sensitive to where you call home. When you get used to a certain area, and are in tune with it, moving out of the neighborhood is unthinkable. That's how I felt about Mt. Pleasant.

I had an appointment to view a house in the neighborhood on the last Sunday in November at 2:30 pm. It was a fine location, but a bit too far east for my liking. What I really wanted, if I could have things my way, was to stay on the same block or at least the same street that I had been living on for the past ten years. But I was feeling resigned to my fate; there were no houses available to rent on my street. I had searched and searched every real estate magazine in North Toronto with no success. I started the day with Sunday mass and offered a rosary to Mother Mary for a house, if it were at all possible, on my street. I should have omitted that 'if' in my rosary request. It was November 26th and I needed to move by December 1st. Like Churchill, I was not about to give up. I still believed that anything is possible with God. After church, I picked up *The Toronto Star* and stopped by my coffee shop. I may as well look through the classifieds, I thought, although I knew that there wouldn't be any new listings so late in the month. Why bother? However, that small still voice told me to go to the rental properties listed in the paper. And there it was! A house was available to rent, a block away on my street. I called on my cell phone and made an appointment to view the house at 1:30 that afternoon. That gave me sufficient time to cancel the other appointment if I liked this house and was accepted as a tenant. I was given the address and told to look for a black Mercedes in the driveway. As soon as I heard the model of the car, I knew that this was meant to be my new home. I had no doubt that this was the right house for me, sight unseen. I had been shown the car in my dream two months prior, and was guided to the right street, with the right house for the right price. It all worked out perfectly. This was serendipity at its finest. It became my new home. Was the Mercedes Benz also mine? In a roundabout way it was. The car owner, who traveled out of town frequently in his position as the sports agent of Pat Quinn, the then manager and coach of The Toronto Maple Leafs hockey team, allowed me the use of his car when he was away three weeks out of the month on business.

June's Birthday Dinner

My intuition led me to spend a very meaningful evening with a special friend one night. June and I had met five years earlier at a message service. It was my second visit to a Spiritualist church. We met over a cup of tea. It would be the first of many cuppas together. There was a twenty-seven year age gap between us, but that didn't matter. We were kindred spirits. We were seekers of divine truth. We had a friendship and bond that transcended age.

She, like Edison, had been raised by Spiritualist parents, and I liked to listen to her stories of communication with them since they passed. It prepared me for my own parents' inevitable crossing. There were times when June's energy and her get up and go put mine to shame. We had more adventures than Abbott and Costello and were just as funny (in my opinion). I learned so much from June every time we chatted. When I told her my spirit guide was a Zulu warrior, she explained the Zulu Wars to me for thirty minutes. She never ceased to amaze me with her vast range of knowledge on a myriad of topics.

June became like a second mother to me. I spent many weekends at her home in East York. We would meditate together, go shopping, see the latest movie, return to her home for dinner, and then tune in to spirit again. If it was too late and the subway was closed, I was often her overnight guest. She told me that she was a 'Ruth,' in a past life, because wherever she went people called her by that name. I listened, but wasn't convinced of it until I witnessed, on three separate occasions, people meeting her for the first time and addressing her as Ruth. We discussed metaphysics daily. We were in touch all day. In fact, we were more in touch then than people with cell phones are today.

Each year we celebrated our birthdays together, mine in mid-March, and June's in late April. In 1987, however, every time we made plans to celebrate her birthday something came up. Every week, her special dinner was postponed, delayed, or we planned a rain check but it never happened. Finally, on June 4th our calendars matched. We were late celebrating but better late than never. It was a lovely spring evening in Toronto and we met in Yorkville and chose a nearby Mexican restaurant. After our meal, we lingered over coffee but passed on dessert. We exited the Colonnade and went window shopping along Bloor Street. We strolled and laughed late into the night until it was time to catch a late train home. I was headed north and June was traveling east. We walked through the underground mall, still wisecracking over the high prices in the shop windows, then June walked with me towards the northbound platform, something she had never done before. Usually we split up, going our separate ways as soon as we entered the subway. I had an overwhelming urge to ask her if I could return to her house and stay overnight. As we approached the northbound train entrance the urge not to part became much stronger. I didn't want to go back to my house that night; I wanted to go to June's instead. Finally, we reached the north entrance, but I didn't want the night to end. After lingering a few more minutes, we said goodnight and planned to see each other at church the next night.

The next morning my phone rang at an exceptionally early hour. I knew bad news was at the other end of the line. I answered to hear one of June's seven sons say hello. That's all I had to hear. I knew immediately that my friend had died in the wee hours of the morning. He was calling to tell me that his mum had passed away during the night of a heart attack. I regretted not insisting that I went home with her and stayed overnight. I would have been there to save her life. My thoughts raced. If only, if only, if only came back to haunt me again. We would have stayed up enjoying a cup of tea. We would have stayed up talking. I would have been with her. I would have called 911. I would have administered CPR. I would have done a lot if only I had been there. But I was not supposed to be there. Once more, I could not change someone else's destiny. I decided to be grateful that June's birthday celebration had been delayed until that night. I realized that was no accident. The consistent postponements and delays had made it possible for me to spend the most meaningful night with my friend. I was grateful that God had allowed me to spend the last night of my friend's life on earth with her, laughing. It was her birthday but it was me who received the best gift.

June has visited me often since crossing over. I am so thankful for each of her visits. Her sense of humor is as sharp as ever. My only regret is that we should have had dessert that night. The next time you are dining out and about to pass on dessert, order the trifle and think of us.

Spirit Saved Me Money

On a happier note, intuition has saved me money. Who doesn't like that? A few years ago I was shopping for an electronic typewriter. Yes, I still used a typewriter. I visited shop after shop and received sticker shock. $600 seemed a bit much for a typewriter. My intuition told me to wait. Don't splurge yet, have patience and wait, Francis whispered. The next morning going out for my daily walk, I noticed my next door neighbor had placed the exact $600 electronic typewriter that I had seen the day before out on the curb for garbage pickup. It was used but that was fine by me. I had no pride or problem carrying it straight away into my living room. That small still voice is ever ready to guide us, guard us, protect us and save us money too. I think of intuition as God and my guardian angel dropping mental hints into my mind. I have learned not to ignore these hints. Intuition, your inner knowing without reasoning, is as true as the North Star. Like God's Love, it is constant and doesn't waiver.

Developing Your Intuition
There are many ways to sharpen your intuition. Here are a few:

The Noah Code
You have probably heard of the books *The Bible Code* and *The Moses Code*. Now try something new – The Noah Code. In 2005, I felt I should buy two of every item when I did my grocery shopping. I wasn't stocking up for a calamity. I wasn't expecting a disaster, but felt the overpowering urge to buy two of every item that was on sale at the supermarket. I didn't know the reason I was doing this, but followed my intuition. I knew I was being guided for some unknown reason that would make sense to me later. It became an inside joke with the cashiers at the store. 'Where's your ark? When's the rain going to start? Will it be forty days and forty nights this time too?' they teased me. As if on cue, every week, a friend or neighbor would drop by, and during the course of their visit they would casually mention an item they needed to buy at the supermarket. Each time I had the item they needed. They were as surprised as me and gratefully accepted the food. Next time you go for your weekly groceries, listen to that small still voice and if it prompts you to buy a few additional items, don't doubt, go with it and see how spirit is using you to help someone else. You'll be combining your intuition with a random act of kindness.

When you're in the market for an expensive new item, whether the latest iPad, a new car, much needed new furniture, television or a designer outfit for an upcoming event, grab the flyers featuring your desired item, or actually go to the store where you intend to make your purchase. Don't rush. Don't be impulsive. Do not let an aggressive sales person hoping for a nice commission pressure you into buying your purchase immediately. Instead, walk around the store at a leisurely pace and let your intuition lead you. If you feel more comfortable tuning in at home, browsing through store flyers, go right ahead. There is no wrong way to use your intuition, except when you ignore it. I know of a woman, who tried this little exercise, and saved $7,000 on her new car. She tells everyone the wait was well worth it. Who doesn't like saving money? You can be next.

God's Hints

God is a generous God. He is especially generous with His hints. He drops them right in front of us, but we must be intuitive enough to pick up on them. For instance, I had a friend back in Pennsylvania who was trying to change careers. No matter how many resumes she sent out or interviews she went on nothing materialized for her.

It was summer and my friend kept receiving invitations to special events. She had received invitations to a charity golf tournament and a hospital fundraiser. She turned down both free tickets. When she received courtesy tickets to a boat cruise I insisted she attend. I volunteered to go with her. It was on this midnight cruise that she met the human resources director of a company where she had wished to work. The director set up an interview and hired my friend within the month. This director had attended both the golf tournament and the fundraiser. My friend and I speculated that if she had gone to either of the two previous events, would she have had the stroke of luck that she had on the cruise? We'll never know, but God never stopped trying to give her the job she dreamed of receiving.

When you pray for guidance you may be moved to take a chance, turn on the television, go online, check on a friend, call a new acquaintance or take a walk at a different time than you normally do. Below is an example that shows how intuition guided me when I needed an emotional pick me up.

A Friend Indeed

One evening I was feeling absolutely drained after listening to a woman who told me how her ex-husband had tried to murder her. What astounded me was that she wanted to know if he would ever marry again. I was thinking to myself, *she should be on her knees thanking God that he did not succeed with his devious plan of murder.* Instead, she was still trying to find out what he was doing in his personal life, which was none of her business. It was time to cut the ties and stop trying to control him.

After she headed home, I began to smudge my living room. I was reflecting on how drained I felt then I thought of a favorite friend, a nurse, who is always a pleasure to be around. I wondered why everyone couldn't be like her. I wished I knew more people like C.

I decided to go for a late walk to the mall, fifteen minutes from my home. Getting out, getting exercise and some fresh air would do my soul good after hearing my neighbor's horror story. It isn't my usual routine to journey out at eight. I have a favorite show that I watch regularly at that time, the amazing *Nancy Grace.* But something told me to go out and forget about the time and crime. I'm glad I did.

I entered the shopping centre through my favorite bookstore and proceeded down the escalator to browse around the stores. The moment I stepped off the escalator, there was my favorite friend, C. We live at opposite ends of the city, but she had stopped by the mall to buy a present for her friend's birthday. The party was in the area. It was a pleasant coincidence that we met. I shouted, 'Am I ever glad to see you,' as I quietly thanked

God for this coincidence. She had no idea how sincerely I meant those words or what bumping into her meant to me that night. Chatting with C. lifted my spirits and renewed my energy. God knew exactly who I needed to see that night, to dissolve the drained feeling which was oppressing me, and He made sure I saw her. The Spirit came down and moved me to the mall. Thank You, Holy Spirit.

When something inside nudges you to break away from your regular routine, just do it. Don't doubt; don't be logical; follow your intuition.

I have a friend who experienced a similar wonderful coincidence, which made an extraordinary difference in her life. One day, after working overtime, she decided to go home via an old two lane highway instead of the faster interstate. She hadn't driven the old road since the interstate went in seven years earlier. She noticed a new restaurant opening that evening a few yards off the two lane road. The featured singer for the grand opening was performing standards from the 1940s and 50s. My friend, a lover of Sinatra, Ella and Tony Bennett, decided to stop and take time from her busy routine to treat herself to one of her favorite things in life. As she walked towards the restaurant door, she thought of her old boyfriend. They used to go dancing to these tunes when they were together fifteen years earlier. Memories of that time came flooding back, but that was then, this is now, she told herself. They had both moved on in their lives and he had moved five states west. She chose a table in the back of the room. After her appetizer arrived, so did her favorite drink sent from a man dining there. How could anyone know her favorite drink was a Long Island Iced Tea? It turned out to be her old boyfriend, the love of her life. Here he was after all that time in the same room. He had recently moved back to the area after living halfway across the country. They spent the evening dancing, just like old times. Their relationship was rekindled and they were married within the year. What made my friend take another road that night? She decided to listen to her intuition. It was 'The Road Not Taken' that made all the difference.

Chapter 6

Meditation

It's been said that when we pray we talk to God; when we meditate, He talks to us. When we pray we ask, and when we meditate we receive His guidance and answers. Choose an area in your home to be your personal sacred space. Make it quiet, blessed, sacred and yours alone. You may wish to place photographs, icons, or statues in the room.

My mediation area includes photographs of Sitting Bull, holy cards of the Blessed Virgin Mary, her Son, Jesus, Sts. Michael and Raphael, and various saints who have answered my prayers since childhood. You may choose to burn candles when you meditate. Candles are a symbol of your intentions and requests going out to God. They also represent God's Divine Light. Each of us carries a spark of the Divine inside of us. Christ said, 'The Kingdom of God is within.' Candles can be a reminder of this as you meditate. Whatever your intention is, here is a small chart to explain candle colors and what they represent.

White:	Spirituality
Black:	Turn away all negativity
Blue:	Healing
Green:	Abundance and prosperity
Pink:	Healing a friendship, good will
Purple:	Psychic ability
Red:	Love
Orange:	Creativity
Silver:	Spirituality
Gold:	Spirituality

I have often advised friends to burn black candles. They are burned to destroy any ill will directed at you and to dissolve negative energy in your home.

If you wish to utilize essential oils with your meditation there are many from which to choose. Lavender, eucalyptus, sandalwood, and patchouli bring relaxation, calmness and serenity to you and your surroundings. There are numerous meditation/relaxation tapes and CDs available to play during your meditation. These can range from Native American drumming/chants, to Indian sitar music, Oriental instrumentals, Gregorian chants or nature sounds. Choose the music that resonates with your soul.

I have digital radio with a nature sounds channel. I enjoy sounds from the Amazon Rain Forest, animals from the Arctic and so on. One night, after midnight, I turned the channel on and began to meditate, not paying any attention to the region featured. Maybe this is a provincial park, I thought. Birds quietly chirped me into the alpha state. I drifted off to the sounds of feathered friends, seeing visions through the Veil. I was going into the theta state of deep meditation when I was abruptly halted by the roar of Leo the lion out of Africa. His ferocious roar came through the surround sound system so loudly it frightened me half to death. My body automatically jumped six inches, as my heart pounded what seemed twice its normal rate. This definitely was not a bird sanctuary but an African safari. I have checked the titles ever since that night to make sure Leo is not on my playlist.

When you meditate you will be shifting your consciousness to another level of brain activity. Beta is the waking state. In 1908, Austrian psychiatrist Hans Berger discovered the alpha state. When you are in the alpha state, you are awake but in a relaxed mode. This is the level you should be in to meditate and visualize. This is the best state to give suggestions to your subconscious mind.

When Thomas Edison couldn't find the solutions in his laboratory he would take time, go into the alpha state, and his answers would come to him after calming his mind in this mode. Whether you are trying to lose weight, quit smoking, find the right career, when you give a suggestion to your subconscious mind, just like Edison's subconscious, yours will accept your suggestion and guide you to the perfect outcome. The expression to 'sleep on it' is not just an old outdated adage. A short period of meditation or nap can often provide the resolutions you are seeking.

A deeper level of relaxation is the theta level, experienced by seers, psychics and those adept in ESP. This is the level your brain would be at to perform remote viewing. The delta level of brain activity is when you are in a deep sleep. In delta, you can experience lucid dreaming and astral travel. You will be conscious and aware that you are dreaming and can even control the direction of your dream as well as the outcome of it.

Begin your meditation by surrounding yourself with God's Divine White Light. From the top of your head to the soles of your feet, imagine His Divine Light enveloping you and protecting you. Quiet your mind, empty it from all thoughts of your busy day. Let go of any anxiety and worry. Change your shallow breathing. Begin inhaling deeply and become aware of the rhythm of your breath. Begin to relax your body starting with your toes, your feet, ankles, legs, knees; proceed to relax your muscles all the way up to your scalp. You will feel the muscles release. Count backwards from twenty. By the time you reach number one, you should be relaxed and ready to tune in.

At first, you may see objects and symbols through a light haze. Take note of the objects and symbols you are seeing. When you see things, this is your clairvoyance developing. You might sense an upcoming event, either a personal one or one on a global magnitude; this is known as clairsentience. Or, you may hear audible messages called clairaudience. No matter how your development begins, if you dedicate fifteen to twenty minutes each morning and evening, your abilities will grow considerably. If you don't see, sense or hear anything at first, don't be discouraged. Continue to practice and with the effort you put in to your meditation your spiritual gifts will come forth. Keep your intentions pure. Use your gifts for the highest and the best for everyone.

Should you choose to meditate with a partner, please choose wisely. Make sure their intentions are pure. It's important that your personal meditation space, where you connect with the Divine, is kept clear of any negative energy. You wouldn't want to invite someone who is overwhelmed with problems to come and meditate with you. I know of someone who felt sorry for a friend and invited them to come and meditate but it proved to be too destructive a vibration. The friend could not forgive a family member and used the time before and after meditation to complain non-stop. My friend learned her lesson and has been meditating solo ever since.

When you meditate you may imagine yourself in your favorite nature setting, a beach, forest, or garden, to gain maximum relaxation. You may choose to meditate on an object that has a spiritual or special meaning for you. Often times, I meditate on a rose. Once in meditation, I heard this message from Francis, 'A rose has more power than an atomic bomb. Love is the strongest vibration. It will transform the world.'

You may choose to focus upon a word, such as love, health, peace, or you may prefer to chant a mantra to yourself. The Sanskrit definition of the word mantra is mind freeing. When you change your thoughts and free your mind you will shift your life.

People worry and ask me if they are meditating in the wrong way. There is no wrong way to meditate. The biggest stumbling block these days seems to be the way of the world. We are rushing everywhere; our schedules are jammed packed with places to go, people to meet, things to do. Some are important, some are not. We are perpetually busy. All meditation requires of you is time and letting go of your busyness.

Auras

What is an aura? Your aura is an energy field that surrounds your physical body. Your aura reflects what is going on with you spiritually and emotionally. This, in turn, is reflected by your physical health. I find very often when someone comes to me with a health issue, the root of their illness is based on a spiritual law which they have broken. It shows in their aura. The two most common laws that are broken are love and forgiveness. Instead of embracing love the person is filled with anger which is aimed at someone in their life. Or, they might be angry and non-forgiving, which is a double edged sword.

A friend stopped by to visit last week and I saw a large amount of black in her aura. I asked her who she was angry with. She replied, 'I'm mad at my mother.' After explaining her weak reason for being mad at her mom, I pointed out how ludicrous her reason was. She finally admitted that it was a rather weak excuse. It wasn't her mother's fault that she didn't have a boyfriend in her life, she was spending sixty hours a week at her job and wasn't making time to meet anyone new. If you're guilty of blaming behavior, like my friend, now is a good time to stop and begin taking responsibility for your actions or lack of action. Your changes will be reflected in your aura.

I keep an eye on my aura by checking it in the mirror every day. The farther out the aura extends, the healthier you are in body, mind and spirit. When it radiates out an inch or lower, it's time for a tune up. Energy that's low will take a toll. When my aura is weak it may be a result of lack of sleep, poor eating habits (dash and dine or too much refined sugar), people around me draining my energy, wasting my time, allowing negative thinking to creep in to my thoughts, or too much caffeine. I know then that it's time to pump up my aura with rest, proper diet, prayer, meditation and chanting.

Yes, even clairvoyants, mediums, seers and mystics must walk the narrow path that Christ and the Hopi Elders spoke of. If anyone is angry with me (because I won't allow them to manipulate me), I pray for them. Likewise, I spend time each day forgiving everyone who has ever hurt me and sending love and forgiveness to them. I don't have any enemies, but if I did I would pray for them like Christ did. I think of Jesus, Nelson Mandela and John Paul II as examples of how I should forgive. If Christ could forgive those who tortured Him, Mandela could forgive his jailers, and John Paul II could meet his would-be assassin in person and forgive him, then I should be able to forgive anyone. Actually, it's not that I *should* forgive – I *must* forgive.

Colors

I am asked often, 'What colors do you see in my aura?' Your aura may have one color or a dominant color mixed with other hues. Here is a list to help you.

Red in your aura represents high energy and vitality.

Yellow in your aura represents health and balance in your life.

Orange represents compassion and kindness. Share these attributes with the people in your life.

Green is the color of healers. Every nurse, doctor, EMT, holistic healer or therapist I have ever met has had a strong emerald hue in their aura. There is no mistaking these altruistic souls who came back to be of service to heal mankind.

Blue represents a spiritual person who possesses a large amount of creativity. I have seen blue in the auras of religious orders, authors, and artists in film and television.

Violet is the color of those souls seeking the mystic. I see it most often in those who have chosen a spiritual path in life instead of running after money. They practices yoga and meditation and have a deeper understanding of spirituality than most people.

White represents the Christ Consciousness. I see this color around priests, monks and ministers. I have seen it emanate around Dr. Zhi Gang Sha in person, in Toronto in 2008, and while watching his live webcasts. Master Sha is a healer whose aura extends more than a foot from his body. Being in his presence is akin to being in the fourth dimension. He is a highly evolved soul and a phenomenal healer.

Chanting

I first learned about the power of certain words and the vibrations they create back in 1994. A neighbor told me a bit of East Indian history and culture. That opened another road for me on my mystical journey. I had read *The Autobiography of a Yogi*, by Paramhansa Yogananda, when I was fifteen. He is the one, along with England's Fab Four, who inspired me to meditate and take the practice of it seriously, not to treat it as just another passing fad. Chanting has allowed me to experience great demonstrations of manifestation and healing. The idea that chanting certain mantras would assist me in attaining my goals in life sounded wonderful and chanting for healing further intrigued me. I was ready to give it a go. Since that initiation, I have chanted daily in English, Hebrew, Latin, Mandarin, Sanskrit and French. I chant each mantra or soul song for eleven or twenty-two minutes. These are the two highest spiritual numbers. Start to chant for eleven minutes and build up to twenty two.

When possible, I chant for several hours and receive abundant blessings, energy and an increase of spiritual gifts. What can you chant for? Anything you like. I chant daily for health and send absent healing to people on my healing list. If you would like to add your name to the list, you can send an email to me at clairvoyantmedium@yahoo.com. Place 'Healing Request' in the subject line. There is no charge for this service. It is free. Absent healing can be sent while you meditate or chant. It's up to you to choose how you would like to send healing. You may visualize sending blue light to the person to the specific area of their body that requires healing. Or, you may chant the word health and picture them receiving Divine White Light into their aura. A very effective chant that I use for financial blessings is Jehovah Jireh, which means God will provide. I chant it believing it, feeling it, knowing it, and then receive my good from God. It never fails. The nice thing about chanting is that you can start at home, at your own pace, without pressure, taking a small amount of time for your spiritual intentions and build up to a larger block of time. You can do it in your meditation area, or while ironing, doing the dishes or putting laundry away. It's totally up to you.

Lost Objects

Decades ago, I was taught by a metaphysician, in the United States, never to panic when I lose something. That was easy for him to say; he had not lost the cherished heirloom my grand-mother had given me. You know when you put something in a special place to be sure you don't lose it then you can't remember where that special place is. That was exactly what I had done. I racked my brain but simply couldn't remember what I had done with my grandmother's antique ring. My teacher explained to me that we can never lose anything. He taught me an exercise which I am sharing with you now. In the event that you lose an article, whether jewelry, a book, money, keys, or your passport, tell yourself it is not lost. Even if you don't believe yourself, keep telling yourself it is not lost. Your subconscious mind knows exactly where the object is. Do not overreact with worry and fear like I did. Calm yourself and sit in meditative silence. Take three deep breathes and ask your subconscious mind to show you where you left your prized possession. I have followed that simple technique for many years and am always able to find the impossible hiding item. I eventually found the ring but first I had to stop being mad at myself. Once I did that and applied myself, I found the ring within five minutes. I have helped people find treasured family photographs, a one of a kind DVD, a large sum of money, toys, and winning lottery tickets. They never lost these items, they just temporarily misplaced them. I guided them with this easy technique. In each case, they found the items they were frantic about losing an hour earlier, within twenty minutes. Your subconscious mind holds the answers, and will always guide you successfully. The secret is to realize and believe that you can never lose anything. You have just temporarily misplaced it.

Of course, there are losses, which occur because you are at a crossroads in your life, whether a job, a relationship or a friendship. Sometimes I am asked if it is okay to end a friendship. In these situations each person has gone through changes, and there is a sense of disconnection between two friends who used to be close. Now, they don't get together as they once did, they don't chat on the phone anymore, they don't meet up for coffee, they no longer have the glue that made them fast friends, or they have each gone off in a different direction in life. I reassure them that it is perfectly okay to say goodbye and to wish each other happiness and break away and not feel an ounce of guilt. Just like we clear out our closet every few months and donate what we no longer use to charity, it can be necessary at times to prune our friendship tree. Your intuition will let you know when it is time to move on.

Exercise: Meeting Your Guides

The Meditation Garden

A popular question people ask me is, 'Can you tell me who my spirit guides are?' Some people have assumed that their deceased mother or father is their spirit guide. I find that to be rare. I do believe our departed loved ones can and do visit us, but spirit guides are usually advanced souls who have chosen to guide us on our life path. They have taken an interest in us for a specific reason. I have had different guides during different phases of my life, and you will too.

If you're interested in connecting with your guides, try this simple meditation.

Once you are in the meditative state, picture yourself in a garden. As you meditate, you will begin to see visitors joining you there. Take note of their clothing, which is the key to letting you know the era they lived in when they were on earth. You may work in medicine and notice someone wearing scrubs. You may work in law enforcement and see that one of your visitors/guides is wearing a uniform from long ago or one from another country. The people who have joined you in your meditation garden are your spirit guides. Your guides may be with you for a short time, some may stay longer, depending on where you are on your path. A guide may come in to help you through a temporary rough patch. You may sense them before you see them. I had a university professor from the UK as one of my guides when I spent a lot of time at the University of Toronto. I sensed him around me but I never saw him. A medium at Britten brought him through one night at the service. When I was a student at The Second City, a recently passed British comedian came through and complimented me on my sketch ideas and comedy writing. Although green is my favorite color, he commented that he hated the color and would not continue working on one film until the green background was abandoned and another color replaced it. I later found out that this was true of Peter Sellers, the soul the medium had brought through. He was not my guide but took a passing interest in my comedy writing. The movie he referred to was *The Party*.

A friend of mine kept smelling fresh flowers whenever she meditated. She could not see her guides but knew the scent was somehow connected to them. She was on the verge of opening a flower shop and took this as a sign that her shop would be successful. The night before her shop launched, she saw her spirit guide, a woman from the 1940s, who showed her a vision of her own flower stand. You will attract guides who have knowledge and experience to assist you with the events and changes facing you. Like attracts like in the universe. Spirit guides follow this law.

Chapter 7

Dreams

Famous Dreamers in the Bible

The Bible is filled with stories of dreams and those skilled in their interpretation. In the Old Testament, Joseph, the eleventh son of Jacob, was sold into slavery by his jealous brothers. As if being a slave wasn't bad enough, Joseph found himself in prison after rejecting the advances of Potiphar's wife. While imprisoned, Joseph accurately interpreted the dreams of two fellow prisoners. One just happened to be the baker to the pharaoh. This led to Joseph finding favor with the pharaoh and being summoned to interpret the ruler's reoccurring puzzling dream.

Gideon was led into battle by a prophetic dream. He successfully defeated the Midianites. King Nebuchadnezzar experienced the same nightmare over and over, but was unable to decipher its meaning. The prophet Daniel explained the true meaning of the king's dream. His belief in and worship of Pagan gods was his great downfall. Nebuchadnezzar refused to repent and suffered insanity until he repented, changed his ways, and saw his kingdom restored.

In the New Testament, the Book of Matthew recalls dreams given to Joseph, the husband of the Virgin Mary. God, through His Angel, guided the Holy Family with dreams. In the first dream, the angel assured Joseph that he should not be afraid to marry Mary.

'But while thinking over these things, behold, an Angel of the Lord appeared to him in his sleep, saying: "Joseph, son of David, do not be afraid to accept Mary as your wife. For what has been formed in her is of the Holy Spirit. And she shall give birth to a son. And you shall call his name Jesus. He shall accomplish the salvation of His people from their sins." Now all this occurred in order to fulfill what was spoken by the Lord through the prophet, saying: 'Behold, a virgin shall conceive in her womb, and she shall give birth to a son. And they shall call his name Emmanuel, which means: God is with us.' Then Joseph, arising from sleep, did just as the Angel of the Lord had instructed him, and he accepted her as his wife. (Matt: 1:21-24).

Joseph was also warned by the angel, in a dream, when Herod was going to slay every male child under the age of two in Bethlehem (Matt: 2:13). Joseph was told in this dream to flee to Egypt and to remain there with Mary and Jesus until further notice. When Herod had died, the angel notified Joseph in another dream.

Then, when Herod had passed away, behold, an Angel of the Lord appeared in sleep to Joseph in Egypt, saying: 'Rise up, and take the boy and his mother, and go into the land of Israel. Those who were seeking the life of the boy have passed away.

And rising up, he took the boy and his mother, and he went into the land of Israel. Then, hearing that Archelaus reigned in Judea in place of his father, Herod, he was afraid to go there. And being warned in sleep, he withdrew into parts of Galilee. And arriving, he lived in a city, which is called Nazareth, in order to fulfill what was spoken through the prophets: 'For he shall be called a Nazarene.' (Matt.2:19-24).

Astral Traveling in Dreams

I hadn't heard from a friend in quite some time. This was back in the day before email, the Internet, and text messages. We kept in touch in one of two ways: through writing letters, as archaic as that may seem, or calling long distance at expensive rates. There had been a four month lull since I had heard from my friend, so I thought it was time to check in with him. Before nodding off to sleep one night, I thought of 'Jack', who lived in

Bucks County, Pennsylvania. That night I had a vivid dream. I dreamed I was at Jack's front door when an angel appeared and said, 'You cannot come in. You must go home. He is going to be a father soon and you do not belong here. Go home.' This angel was no cutesy cupid; he meant business. He wasn't one bit friendly towards me but was very stern. He was not about to allow me past the front door to visit my friend. I turned away from the door and woke up instantly. What a dream. That was too real to be just a dream, I told myself. That was always my first reaction upon waking from a lucid dream in the middle of the night. I decided to call Jack later in the day and went back to sleep. I rang Jack just after lunch. Recognizing my voice, he excitedly exclaimed, 'I'm going to be a father!' I was not surprised in the least. The authority with which the angel had spoken to me in my dream had convinced me it was the truth, revealed now, nine hours later, by the proud papa to be. I have had truths revealed to me in dreams since childhood. I was tempted to tell Jack, 'I already knew you're preparing for fatherhood, because an angel informed me at your house last night, in a dream,' but for once I kept quiet and let him have his moment. I offered my congratulations, wished him and the missus the best and wondered if I would ever meet an angel like that again. I did. I met two with the same no-nonsense attitude years later in Toronto.

Predicting Pregnancy
A few years later, in Toronto, I had a vivid dream of my friend Sylvie W. expecting a baby. I had to call her and see if my dream was accurate. She was well aware of my clairvoyant abilities because I had found her lost engagement ring, not once, but twice. Sylvie was engaged and wore her diamond ring proudly. One day she misplaced the ring and called me for help finding it. Over the phone, I quietly asked for God's help. Immediately, my mother came through and showed me a vision that her ring

was in the crease of her futon in the living room. I relayed Mom's message to Sylvie and suggested that she go to the living room and shake the futon. No, she insisted, it wasn't there. She assured me that she had left the ring in the bathroom, while showering. She was certain that her future and her diamond ring were now floating in the Toronto Sewerage System. I'm not one to argue with a friend, but I kept seeing the ring pinched in the crease of the futon. Sylvie thanked me, but her mind was made up – the ring was gone. My mom begged to differ.

Two weeks went by. Feeling sad, Sylvie called me to commiserate about her lost engagement ring. I didn't see anything new with the ring situation. My mother came through and insisted that Sylvie immediately shake that ring out of the living room futon. Finally giving in, Sylvie put the phone down, went into the living room, shook the futon, and I heard, 'Oh! Betsy Balega!' When God, one of His Angels or my *dead* mother comes through, I listen. I trust in Him, His Angels and my mom more than anyone else on earth. Two more weeks passed and I received another call from Sylvie. Her diamond ring had vanished again. Déjà vu loves popping up in my life. Once more the ring was found with clairvoyance and the help of my mother. Sometimes I feel like I should be working in Macy's Lost and Found Department.

Now it was my turn to call Sylvie and see how accurate my dream had been. I got right to the point – was she expecting? No, she wasn't pregnant, but she did have a bladder infection. She was visiting the bathroom several times during the night. I assured her that she had no bladder infection; she had a baby onboard. She agreed to disagree with me. She had a doctor's appointment the next day and was going to be treated for a bladder infection.

I decided it was time to be Dr. Betsy. I insisted that she didn't have any type of infection; she was pregnant. I knew this because I had dreamed it. The dream had been so specific and so real that it was definitely a precognitive dream. No, she counter-insisted, there was no baby on the way. I asked Sylvie to have the doctor include a pregnancy test, just in case, and she said she would just to prove how wrong I was. The results wouldn't be available for another ten days, but I made her promise to call me as soon as she got them. Eleven days passed and no call came from Sylvie. My curiosity was getting the best of me. The suspense got to me and I called her on day twelve. 'Sylvie, what were your test results? Tell me, tell me,' I asked. 'Betsy Balega, you already know,' was her reply. Yes, my dream had been 100% accurate. Keep track of your dreams, especially lucid ones. God is talking to you in them, preparing you for your future.

Meeting the Dead

I have had clients relate stories to me of meeting and talking with their dead mother, father, siblings and friends in their dreams. They wonder if they are losing their minds, or if it is possible to communicate with those who have crossed over to the next dimension when they are asleep. My answer has been, 'You are not losing your mind. You are not crazy, and yes, it is possible to meet loved ones between the two worlds, when you sleep.' The First Nations People call this dream walking. You and I call it astral travel. Whatever we call it, it is real. It is when your spirit/soul leaves your physical body during sleep. The soul is connected, by a silver cord, from the solar plexus, to your body, when you go traveling in the spirit. I have seen this cord many times in my nightly travels. It is when the cord is severed, that a person dies and crosses over.

My teacher cautioned us to be careful while traveling on the astral plane. If you go roaming too far you may not be able to find your way back. That's why I did not roam far or go off exploring the astral realm the first night I found myself standing outside of my physical body in Philadelphia. She also warned us about malicious spirits who may intentionally attempt to cut the cord and you won't be able to come back if they succeed. She cautioned against leaving your body to allow a spirit to enter and channel information through the use of your physical body. They may not want to leave, thus creating chaos. Chaos does not come from God but the lower regions of the spirit world. Peace, love, harmony and order in the universe are from God.

Deceased Neighbor Told Me that My Mother Would Join Her

In the fall of 1984, I experienced another lucid dream. This dream was of a neighbor, who lived around the block from our house on Franklin Street. My mother was the brownie scout leader, of the St. Anne Troop, at St. Ed's. She became friends with Pauline H., when Pauline's daughter, Karen, joined the brownie troop. Pauline crossed over to the Higher Side of Life in the early 1970s. Years later we briefly met again in spirit. In my dream we were standing in front of a friend's house, on South Shamokin Street. I recognized Pauline instantly and knew she had crossed over. I wondered why we were meeting. What did she want to tell me? She said one sentence to me, mind to mind: 'Don't worry, Betsy, your mother will be with me soon.' And then I woke up. I knew instinctively what Pauline was telling me, but in my heart I was hoping it wasn't going to happen. I knew I could not stop it – my mother would die soon. When my mother was hospitalized, other family members looked forward to her coming home, but I knew she was going to join Pauline on the Other Side of Life and I never revealed this dream to my mother or to anyone in my family.

In my dream I was surprised that Pauline remembered me. I wondered why she had made the effort to warn me. It was very kind of her and I was glad that she did. This dream has meant a lot to me. It showed me that I wasn't forgotten. It showed me that someone cared and loved me and was concerned about how I would be feeling when my mother's appointed time arrived to go into spirit. I knew what good friends Pauline and my mother were. Pauline wanted to reassure me that their friendship would continue on the Other Side. My mom definitely wasn't going to be alone. There were friends and relatives waiting to greet her and help her to adjust to living in the spirit. This dream reinforced the power of love to me. Across the universe someone cared enough to come back to comfort and reassure me seven months before this sad event occurred. I will always be grateful to Pauline for her love and compassion.

Nana Knew the Lottery Numbers

Around the same time, I had a dream of my nana. She had crossed over on October 28, 1974. In this lucid dream, we met in a beautiful garden. This garden is well known to people who have traveled in the spirit to meet the dead in their dreams. Like Pauline, Nana was brief and to the point. She gave me some numbers to play in the lottery. She did this telepathically. She was very clear that the numbers were not for me, but for my mother, in Pennsylvania. I had the intense feeling, in my dream, that if I did not call my mother the next day and give her these numbers, my nana would be extremely angry with me.

My nana and I had been very close in life; at times we were more like a mother and daughter than a grandmother and granddaughter. A mean word was never exchanged between us and anger from Nana was unthinkable. Just the thought of her being mad at me upset me in my dream.

When I awoke, I easily remembered the numbers. I called my mother that night and told her my dream along with the numbers for her to play in Pennsylvania. Other mothers might have thought that their daughter had gone off the deep end, but my mom was used to my sixth sense by now and took me and my dream seriously.

I spent the next Saturday afternoon shopping for a new answering machine. Returning home after five, I connected the machine. All I needed was to have someone call me to see if I had connected it properly. I tried calling several friends to help me test the phone, but no one was at home that afternoon, so I walked to the corner and called myself from a pay phone. I left a test message and returned home to see if the machine had recorded it. To my surprise, the light was blinking not once, but twice. I had received two calls. Gee, isn't that always the way, I thought; step outside for five minutes and a friend calls. Where were they ten minutes ago when I needed them to call?

I wondered who my first caller was. To my surprise it was my mother. She left a message stating that the lottery numbers I had given her had been correct. I called Mom back and we had one of our mother/daughter talks about dreams that aren't just dreams, but are so much more. She told me our next door neighbor, Violet, wanted to know if I had any more hot tips to play. I asked Mom if Violet knew who gave me the hot tips. Mom assured me that she did and was perfectly fine with accepting additional numbers from Nana Balega, or anyone else from the Other Side, who wanted to share some more good luck in Shamokin.

Closer Than That

In January 1985, I treated myself to a private reading with the incomparable medium, Vince van Limbeck. If you haven't met Vince, at one of the churches in Toronto, perhaps you have seen him in action at Lily Dale, New York, during the season. Lily Dale is a Spiritualist community in northwestern New York State. Vince is one of eleven children, six of whom have Second Sight. During my reading, Vince asked me which female I was trying to contact on the Other Side. 'No one,' I responded. I wasn't *trying* to reach anyone. I didn't need to *try*. I saw my grandmothers all the time. Either they appeared in person or in my dreams. I had no problem connecting with them. We shared a strong connection in life that carried over after their deaths.

'No, *closer* than that,' Vince remarked. *There is no one closer*, I thought. So, I simply answered, 'No one. I'm not trying to reach anyone.' I let it go at that and forgot about his comment.

Looking back now, I realize I received Vince's message like I had received the dream of Pauline, to prepare me for my mother's death on July 4th of that year. I'm certain Vince knew it was my mother whom I would be trying to contact in August. That is why he referred to them as closer than my grandmothers. He too showed compassion by not blurting out, 'Your mother is going to die.' I would make contact with Mom in August. That's the difference I have noticed between psychics and trained or natural mediums. Psychics may come out with the blunt truth, but the mediums I have met soften the blow and carefully word a message in a milder manner. I had made a tape of my reading with Vince. I played it for my family after my mother's funeral Mass. I finally shared my dream of Pauline H. that day with my Aunt Marie, to let her know why I never believed my mom would recover and come back home.

I know of a psychic who told a client that her husband, her brother-in-law, and her son would all die within a year and a half of the reading. The woman began to worry the moment these words came out of the reader's mouth. I believe a medium would have advised the woman to take more time and spend it with her family, urging her to make more memories together while there was time. Unfortunately, the psychic's visions were accurate; all three males died within the next eighteen months.

Meeting an Old Friend
In the summer of 2007, my dreams took me to Seattle Airport. In that dream, an old friend came up to me, looked me in the eyes and said, 'Hi Betsy, it's me, Ron P.' He didn't have to tell me his name, I recognized him instantly. He turned and walked away. I woke up abruptly and once more, the sense that this was more than a dream permeated my thoughts. Where was I? Where was

I? What airport was that? I questioned. I couldn't remember. Francis responded immediately, 'It was Seattle.' *Seattle*, I thought, then fell fast asleep.

The dream was on my mind all day. What a dream; it was so real. I wondered what it meant. I hadn't seen my friend in twenty years. Why would I dream of him? Would I bump into him soon? We don't live in the same city. When Ron lived in Toronto I witnessed his uncanny ability to tell me of someone from Vancouver, whom he hadn't seen in several years, and then run into the person the next day in Toronto. Was it going to happen to us? To add more intrigue, that night in meditation, my mother came to me and said, 'Portland, Oregon.' She told me I would see Ron's name and number show up on my caller ID but she didn't give the exact date. I wrote everything down in my journal. The Seattle Airport, Portland, Oregon; I had never been to either city but knew there was a reason for this lucid dream and my mother's messages. Sometimes the smallest events can lead to the biggest surprises in our lives.

Soon after my mother's visit, two old friends stopped by in spirit. They spontaneously appeared in my living room. John had been in business with Ron and Rocco was Ron's cousin. These two old pals came to confirm my mother's messages. I would be hearing from Ron soon. Whenever my mother gives me a message I believe her; now I had two friends agreeing with her and I believed all three. If there's anything I have learned about spirit friends, it is that whether they appear in my dreams, or appear in person, they don't lie.

Two months later, the name Ron P. and his telephone number showed up on my caller ID just as my mother had told me. I had missed his call. We connected by email a few days later. I had to ask if he had been in Portland the previous year. His answer didn't surprise me in the least. He had been working in California, headed north to Portland, and while there, he had decided to return to Ontario. Already knowing the answer to my next question, I inquired about John and Rocco. He wrote back, 'They both died. I miss them very much.' I informed him that they had paid a visit and foretold his call. He took this all in stride, as he has known since we met that I am a clairvoyant medium. Often times, people tell me, 'I lost my mother.' My standard reply is always the same: 'You didn't lose your mother, because she knows where to find you.' Your friends can find you too. Somehow, someway, they'll connect with you. John and Rocco knew I was the channel for them to connect with Ron. It was the power of love that kept the four of us connected through the Veil.

Tap into that power every day to receive your special surprises.

Exercise

Here is a very simple exercise to connect with your departed family members and friends. Take their photographs and place them beside a lit candle. Place a vase of flowers, keeping it a safe distance from the flame, next to the photographs. This will draw your loved ones to you. You may sense their presence, or smell your grandmother's signature perfume, or your grandfather's pipe tobacco. It's very simple and very effective.

Another exercise is to sit and go through your family photo album. As you sit and reminisce, reflect on the happy times you shared together. Your relatives will come and sit beside you and remember with you. I do this exercise on birthdays, anniversaries and at Christmas. You may receive spontaneous messages as you go through your albums on your important dates and during the holidays you celebrate.

As you dream, your soul is reviewing what is going on in your life. Your dreams are just one way you can connect with God and receive His input.

Everyone dreams every night. If we didn't dream we would eventually go insane. Some of my friends have difficulty remembering their dreams. This is easily resolved. If you have trouble recalling your dreams, perform a little self talk before you go off to sleep. Tell yourself you will remember your dreams, you look forward to receiving your dreams, and the messages they will give you. Ask your angels to help you remember them. They're happy to help you. Place a pen and paper on your night stand so when you awake in the middle of the night you can turn your light on and jot down the dream you had.

It's very common for angels and guides to deliberately interrupt your sleep and wake you, to make sure you remember a particular dream. When this has occurred in my life, it proved to be a very important message that spirit did not want me to miss. Also, note the time of your dream, if possible. I experienced several months when I consistently awoke at 4:44 in the morning. Not just the dreams, but the time was of significance, as 4:44 is the number of angels. It happened to be a very trying time in my life, but I confidently believed my angels were telling me not to worry. Once more they were right.

Attempting Astral Travel

If you want to connect with someone on the astral plane as you sleep, think of that person for five minutes before nodding off to dreamland. Imagine what you would say to them. Think of the conversation you would have with them if they were sitting beside you. If there is a problem to be resolved, imagine a happy resolution coming during sleep. Ask God and your angels for Divine protection as you travel. Do your traveling for the highest good. Don't attempt any action that would create pain for another person.

Exercise

This type of astral travel is also known as remote viewing. My teacher, Mary, explained to us one evening how the consciousness can leave the physical body and travel anywhere in the universe. Before she left for class that evening, she had placed five items on her dining room table. The twelve of us students were to travel to Mary's house, by projecting our consciousness there, and report back what items she had placed on the table. Her home was several miles from her classroom. We looked at each other wondering if we were at the level to perform such a detailed task. My thoughts ran along the lines of, you have got to be kidding me. I can't do this. Surely, you jest. But, as we relaxed, counted backwards from twenty, I let go of my doubt and attempted to become a psychic snoop. I surprised myself and everyone in the class by naming all five objects on Mary's table. This reinforced to me that I should never doubt, but accept exactly what I see with my spiritual eyes, no matter how illogical it may seem at the time.

If you would like to travel outside of your body, while awake, projecting your consciousness to another part of the city, or world, begin with getting into your meditation mode. Relax, breathe deeply, relaxing your body from the soles of your feet to the top of your head. Count backwards from twenty until you reach your total relaxation point. Then, focus on the location you would like to be at in your mind. Take your time and don't rush yourself. Keep your focus until you begin to see your way around your desired location.

You may smell different aromas, or sense someone you know being there in the physical. You may hear a specific type of music being played or hear a conversation. This exercise is not meant to teach you how to invade another's privacy; it's to teach you that you have more than your five senses at your fingertips. Again, make sure your intention is pure when you set out on your astral adventures.

I taught this technique to a friend, who later used it to check on her daughter when a severe ice storm had knocked out all power in Quebec where her daughter lived. She was concerned for her daughter and her family's safety. She went into meditation and traveled, using her consciousness, to see how her daughter was coping during the storm. She saw the family cooking with their wood fireplace and her two granddaughters playing a game of Chinese checkers. Two days later, after power had been restored, her daughter confirmed everything her mother had seen using remote viewing.

A little note here on intuition; when her daughter and son-in-law were house hunting, her son-in-law preferred a condo with no fireplace. Her daughter insisted they purchase property that had a working wood fireplace 'just in case of an emergency'. Her 'just in case' came in handy that winter.

I like to use this exercise when I hear of disasters. First, I will send Francis to go to the site and take angels along with him to calm people who were caught off guard by the quake, or whatever disaster has hit. Then I will meditate and project love and compassion to everyone at the location. I project my consciousness if the disaster has hit during the night. Experiencing an earthquake or flood is scary enough during the day, let alone in darkness of night.

Chapter 8

Wishes are Prayers - Coincidences Are Confirmation

As I wrote this book, I became surrounded by wishes coming true. Coincidences occurred on a daily basis. I joked with friends that God had a wire tap on me or a Spiritual GPS. I would no sooner think of what I would like to show up in my life, than it would happen within twenty-four hours. That's what happens when you're in touch with God. Keep the line open.

My Christmas Wish

I learned at a young age that wishes can come true. Our church had, and still has, a manger installed beside the rectory every Christmas Season. When I was nine, I had a deep desire to hold Jesus from the manger. Every time I walked by the church or stopped in to make a visit (with my friends at lunch time), I made my wish. On the weekends, when our family went to Nana's for dinner, I'd make my wish as we drove by St. Ed's. I knew logically that there was no way I'd be able to hold Baby Jesus but I didn't stop wishing. The manger was set up the first week of Advent and was returned to storage after the Feast of the Epiphany. I had no idea how I would ever get to hold the Infant, but I kept wishing.

One Friday afternoon in December, a knock came on the door of our classroom. Sister Joseph Therese met Father Greycheck at the door. They had a brief conversation. The next thing I knew, I was told that Father wanted to speak with me. My only thought was that my mom had died and Father was going to break the bad news to me. I held my breath and went out into the hallway. He explained he had adapted a play and asked if I would accept the role of the Virgin Mary. The rehearsals would be held after school. The play would be performed the week before Christmas. In my role as Mary I would present the Christ Child to a humble altar boy. Where was the Christ Child going to be found? Father was going to use the Baby Jesus from the church manager, of course. After receiving my Christmas Wish, I realized that I had not prayed to hold the statue of Jesus; I had just wished for it. God knew what was in my heart. Remember that the next time you make a wish. I received my wish. You can receive yours. Keep your heart and intention pure as you wish. Let logic out of it. God is bigger than that. Just as there seemed to be no way for me to get my Christmas Wish, the way appeared. God finds the way when there is no way. He'll find the way for you.

God Gave Me a Mustang

Ten years later, I made another silent wish. Walking to the library one day, I passed by a new Ford Mustang. It belonged to a woman in the neighborhood who had it painted pink. As I passed by, I silently told God 'that's the car for me, but I don't want my car to be pink.' Then I got specific and told God exactly what kind of Mustang I wanted. It had to be a Grande. That was my favorite style – no Mach 1 for me. But, unlike this lady's car, my Mustang did not have to be brand new. It was okay with me, if it was an older model. A 1969 model would be fine with me. I wanted an automatic on the floor. My Mustang was to be a dark forest green, and it should have British racing stripes on the sides, white with gold pinstripes. I knew exactly what I wanted. I could see it. I placed my order with God. I only told Him once. I knew He heard me. He wasn't deaf. He was listening to me. I never asked; I told Him what I would like to receive. I never mentioned my request to anyone.

Eight months later, my dad told me he had picked out a car for me. He and Mom would take me to test drive the car on

Friday night. He never mentioned details about the car and I didn't ask for any. I trusted my dad's knowledge of cars and his good judgment whenever he bought one.

Friday night, we drove to the dealership. That was the first time I saw my 1969, deep forest green, Grande Mustang, with British racing stripes of white and gold on both sides. Yes, it had an automatic on the floor. It was everything I had casually asked God for last summer. I couldn't have asked for more. My earthly father and my heavenly Father both came through for me. I trusted the two of them and I still do. I shared this story with my parents a few years later. They were astonished that I had received exactly what I had asked God for without mentioning it to them. He does work in mysterious ways. We knew it was no accident that the Mustang found me. People have wanted to buy my Mustang, but I have passed on all offers. It is a constant reminder to me how consistently great God is.

Surrounded by Coincidences

As I mentioned, coincidences happen to me on a daily basis. One day I arrived at the coffee shop bright and early to dig into the *Toronto Star* and see what was going on in the city. As I met Frank, the manager, I exclaimed, 'Home Sweet Home,' for some inexplicable reason. I didn't know what had come over me to shout out the phrase; maybe it was my fondness for the staff. I had gotten to know a few employees, as best one can when living in the city, and the shop was a tiny oasis from the impersonal service you sometimes encounter at a counter. When I sat down at my table, I opened the *Star* to the Life section to read the headline, 'Home Sweet Home'. I knew God was saying hello.

Three years later, a woman asked me why she was still on earth. Her daughter had died and she wanted to be with her on the Other Side of Life, instead of being kept here on earth. She felt there was no reason for her to remain in the physical. I told her that some days I wake up and ask God the same questions:

Why am I still here? What do You want me to do for You today? How can I serve You, Your world and the people in it? I told her we are still here because our work is not completed. If it was, God would take us home. Then I added, 'We are here to give people hope sweet hope.' I had no idea why I said that phrase or where it came from. I made it up, or somebody made it up for me, and made the words come out of my mouth. The Spirit had come down on me again.

The next morning, I arrived at my coffee shop at my usual 6 am. It was time for my daily routine of coffee and the *Toronto Star*. I opened the paper to the Condo Section, to read the headline, 'Hope Suite Hope'. For this to happen once was enough to make me believe, without a doubt, that God watched and guided me. For it to happen twice, was a solid sign that God takes an interest in the smallest things I do and say to people. He guides my actions and words. He cares for me and all the people who are my friends and associates. If He is interested in small affairs imagine how He wants to guide our important decisions in life.

My dad loved liver and onions. He liked to remind me that even though I didn't eat this combo, The Sleeping Prophet, Edgar Cayce, recommended eating it once a week. I was thinking of my dad one morning and felt him very close. It was time to start my day with my usual cup of java and the newspaper. I opened the paper to the Food Section to be greeted with a large photo of liver and onions along with a headline touting its benefits. A few days later, while doing a puzzle, one of the answers was foie gras (the fatty liver of a duck or goose). The next thing I knew I was seeing headlines everywhere about foie gras. Quebec was experiencing a foie gras crisis. Foie gras was getting as much press as Paris Hilton. Restaurants featuring foie gras sent me their flyers in the mail. At every turn I was met by foie gras. A friend was passing through my neighborhood and stopped by to give me some foie gras. This had to be a hello

113

from my earthly father, who was saying hello in his own funny way.

The night before I submitted this manuscript, a friend and I went to my coffee shop and began to discuss world affairs. My friend happened to make a comment about the three wise monkeys who see no evil, hear no evil and say no evil. Twenty minutes later, a carnival truck came by our window towing six foot tall fiberglass monkeys behind it. They were not the well known trio of monkeys, but we both thought it was no coincidence that they just happened to pass the window so soon after his comment.

When coincidences happen to you, even the silly ones, think of them as God talking to you and telling you, you are exactly where you are meant to be. You are on time, on target and on the right track. He is in touch with you. That's no coincidence. It is confirmation, affirmation from Him, and a personal connection with Him. Your Heavenly Father is saying hello. Watch when you suddenly blurt out words, or a sentence, for no known reason. I was taught that this is your angel guiding you, or the Holy Spirit inspiring you.

Botticelli

Christmas is one of the most spiritual times of the year. The past two Christmases brought lovely coincidences into my life. In early December 2008, I turned on my television to watch a fascinating documentary about artists. Botticelli, one of my favorites, was featured. The next evening, a friend came by for dinner and surprised me with a lovely bottle of wine. What kind of wine did she bring? It was Botticelli, of course.

The next day, I had a strong craving for chocolate, so I trekked through the snow to the local drugstore to buy some chocolates. I had no particular brand in mind; I just wanted to satisfy my craving. I walked down the candy aisle comparing milk with dark chocolate. Should I buy a box of chocolates or just a candy bar? I couldn't decide. So many choices should make my choice simple I thought but it wasn't. I never had trouble making up my mind. I had my favorites but just wasn't in the mood for them. I turned at the end of the aisle where a new display caught my eye. It was the bright blue wrappers that attracted my attention. I walked over to read the wrapper. It was Boticelli Chocolate. That was the end of my indecision.

After Christmas, I decided it was time to buy a picture to cover the bare wall in my living room. There would be lots of Boxing Day Sales with great bargain prices. I had no idea what type of painting I wanted for the wall. I had no particular color scheme in mind. I'll go window shopping, I thought, and when I see the right picture I'll know it. On my way out to go shopping, I took the side stairwell instead of the elevator. I usually took the elevator but something seemed to say, take the stairs. At the side door was a nice picture with a sign beside it that read, 'Free for the taking.' It was perfect for my living room wall. It was the right size and the right price. I wasn't going to argue. I gratefully picked up the painting. The picture looked familiar to me. I'd have a better look when I took my reading glasses out of my purse. The artist's name was right on the tip of my tongue but I just couldn't place him. I took the painting under my arm and cancelled my shopping spree. I was doubly grateful the freebie had also saved me a trip out into the frigid weather. When I got the picture inside my apartment, I took a closer look at it, this time wearing my reading glasses. No wonder it looked familiar. It had been featured in the documentary I had watched earlier in the month. It was *The Birth of Venus* by Boticelli. My intuition had led me exactly to what I wanted, while saving me time and money.

Christmas Cheer
The next year, Christmas spawned a whole new set of coincidences. They all involved food, chocolate and wine. How good

does it get? Tres bon. It was time to go grocery shopping for the holidays. It was snowing furiously so I decided to put my shopping off for a few days but I knew I couldn't let it go too long. It was already December 16th. I had just one more week before Christmas to get myself moving, motivated and fill up my cupboards. I made my shopping list and, like Santa, I checked it twice, careful not to forget anything. One item I had to stock up on was peanut butter for my favorite cookies, and Melba toast was a must for the pate. I also had run out of dish detergent so that was another must item. I'd get around to my shopping tomorrow for sure I told myself.

That night, I received a surprise call from my coffee shop. Someone had left a package for me which I could pick up anytime. It would be safely tucked away, behind the counter. All I had to do was ask one of the staff for it. I told Anna, the manager, I would get the package the next day when I did my grocery shopping. The morning of the 17th I made my way to the coffee shop. A huge eco friendly grocery bag, brimming over with a variety of groceries, was brought out for me. Inside were the exact items I had written on my shopping list. How could that happen? What a wonderful coincidence. I called my friend Maggie, and asked what had possessed her to buy so many groceries for me. If I hadn't had help it would have taken me three trips to get all the food home. She stated she 'just had a feeling' to pick up a 'few' items for me. It was also my dad's birthday. He might have had a hand in this coincidence, making sure I had plenty of Melba toast for my foie gras. I shared my 'coincidence' with friends who stopped by that holiday season, and enjoyed the treats made with Maggie's grocery gift. On the morning of December 24th, a friend wanted to come by and wish me a Merry Christmas after lunch. She asked me if I needed any groceries. The supermarket was close by and she could pick up items on her way over to my place. I told her all I needed was milk, bread and butter. I still had Maggie's groceries overflowing in my cupboards. No problem; she'd be at my apartment by two and bring the basics. After we hung up, I regretted that I hadn't asked her to pick up a bottle of red wine to share a holiday toast. Then I got to thinking; some Lindt truffles would have been good to add to the mini list. I had another chocolate craving and this time I knew I was craving Lindt truffles in the blue wrappers. When my friend arrived at two, she had the basics I had requested, and added, 'Oh, and I brought a bottle of red wine for you and some Lindt Truffles.' I opened the second bag and was delighted to see the wrappers were blue. There was an unspoken energy working around me this Christmastide.

By the beginning of January, it was time for me to go buy my own groceries and stop receiving special deliveries from my friends in supernatural ways. Although, I must admit I enjoyed their surprises. The first weekend of the New Year, my best friend came by for his birthday lunch. My Christmas coincidences weren't over yet. He arrived with seven bags of groceries and two bottles of California Red for me. Although it was Ron's special day, once again, I was receiving more gifts. What an abundant season it had been, filled with coincidences and super surprises.

Coast to Coast AM

I became a 'Coastie', a fan of Coast to Coast AM, America's #1 late night Paranormal Talk Radio Show, in 1996. It was on Coast that I first learned about The Ghost Dance. The Ghost Dance is a Native American Ceremony which was outlawed by the United States Government back in the 1800s. The dance was performed to bring back the One who would save the Native Peoples. I longed to know more about The Ghost Dance. A few weeks later that still small voice inspired me to take a trip to The Annex area in Toronto. This neighborhood includes the University of Toronto and many specialty shops. On my leisurely walk I came upon a book bin on the sidewalk. The first book that caught my eye was *The Ghost Dance* by James Mooney. My logical mind was saying how can this be? The real me was saying thank You Spirit. God, you never fail to answer me and my wishes. You never fail to amaze me. This was a special coincidence as I often feel Native American and Canadian spirits with me.

Three weeks later, after reading the first half of *The Ghost Dance*, I wished that I could learn history from the Native American's point of view, instead of from those who had won all the wars. Spirit inspired me to return to the Annex. I followed this divine inspiration and found myself at the same book bin. I hit pay dirt again. This time my purchase was *Native Time: An Historical Time Line of Native America* by Lee Francis. This was exactly what I wanted to read. I felt God and my Native Spirit Guides were both talking with me and leading me. There was no doubt about it.

RAK's Trigger Coincidences

Are you ready to experience coincidences in your life? Have you ever performed a Random Act of Kindness or, as they are commonly known, an RAK? I'm sure you have. There are opportunities presenting themselves to us on a daily basis, if we are aware and ready to respond to them. One Sunday at brunch, I was in the giving mood. I picked up the bill and paid for my friend's meals. I felt it was the right thing to do. It felt like the right time. My friends thanked me and asked if there was anything they could do for me in return. The only thing I needed was a pair of red leather shoes. I had bought a red dress and a purse to match the day before. Why bother them with my shopping story? We weren't going out to a shoe sale at the moment. No, there was nothing I needed, I told them, thanks for asking.

My friends and I left the restaurant and headed over to the

mall to see a movie. It was our favorite way to escape the heat and humidity in the middle of August. After the show, I returned home and found a package at my front door. The box contained a pair of red leather shoes from a friend who had just returned from two weeks holiday. Her note stated that she had been out shopping while in Boston and felt the urge to buy these shoes for me. She hoped I liked them. My RAK came back to me the same day. It returned in the form of the only item I wanted. I was speechless but grateful. Aren't God and His Universe great? I think so too.

RAK Ideas

Here are some ideas to get you started with your random acts of kindness:

1. Pay for the coffee of the person behind you in line.
2. Give business to your competitors when they need it.
3. Let someone who is in a rush go ahead of you in line.
4. Let the cashier keep your change for the next person who might need it.
5. Adopt a family at Christmas and be their Secret Santa.
6. Run an errand for anyone who is housebound.
7. Baby-sit for a couple who need an evening out.
8. Collect toys and donate them all year long.
9. Make a donation of clothing, or your time, to a shelter.
10. Make dinner for a shut-in.

I am sure you have your own ideas. Be creative, be generous, be grateful and all your good will return to you effortlessly.

Appreciation and Gratitude

Did you know that what you focus on will expand? Have you ever asked, when things are going wrong, what else could possibly happen? only to have something worse happen almost instantly? This is not your imagination playing tricks on you. This is Universal Law. Thoughts, attitudes and words have a life of their own. That is why I can't stress enough how important it is for you to guard your thoughts, attitudes and words. Keep them positive at all times.

It's no secret that appreciating what you have will bring more of it into your life. Gratitude is an attitude to nurture and grow. The more grateful you are, and the more thanks you give to God, the more you will receive from Him. Whenever I receive an answer to a prayer, I think of the ten lepers in the New Testament. Jesus cured all ten, but only one returned to say thank you to Him. I think of myself as the one who returns to Christ, again and again to thank Him. This act of thanking God is a spiritual magnet that draws even more abundance into my life. It shows up in other ways, besides money. Practice thanking God daily and you'll receive more of His rewards and blessings.

Exercises

At the first of the month, write out your Wish List for the next four weeks. Wish for whatever you want to manifest in your life. It may be small, like the two books I wanted; or it may be large, like my car. It may be for the right job to come to you or a long awaited promotion. You may be wishing for the right relationship. Write it down. Look at your list every night before you go to sleep and send your wishes out to God. Read it in the morning during your prayer time. Keep your intentions pure and your heart filled with gratitude and expect your wishes to manifest in your life soon.

Make a list of past coincidences in your life. Go back to your childhood, if you can, and you'll see a pattern emerge. Start to keep track of the coincidences in your life now. Keep a Gratitude Journal and write every day at least ten things in your life that you are grateful for and appreciate. The more you express gratitude, the more you will receive. It may sound simple but read your list and appreciate what is already in your life. As you embrace appreciating what you have, more good will automatically come to you. I have my ten before ten list that I write daily. Every day before 10 am I write and say out loud ten things I am grateful for. I add ten more before 10 pm.

Chapter 9

Getting in Touch with God

Where Is God?

At five years old, I learned that God is omnipresent. That's a big word for a little girl. He is everywhere. He is not just in churches, chapels and cathedrals. I feel His Presence everywhere. Do you? You can if you remember He's right beside you, not in a galaxy far, far away. It's up to you and me to acknowledge Him. When we do, we are in touch with God. If we seek Him, He will make His Presence known to us.

This is the Wired Generation. Who can deny that? Every time I open a newspaper or turn on the television, I'm bombarded with mega ads for iPods, iPads, iPhones, Smart Phones, Apps, MP3 Players, X-Boxes, Laptops, LCD TV's, Plasma TV's, Video Recorders, and accessories to go along with all of these products. Have you noticed the more connected we are, the more disconnected we have become? The family dinner hour seems to have gone the way of the Dodo Bird. Everyone is rushing. Everyone is in such a hurry. No one seems to have enough time in the day, or gets enough sleep at night. Even former President Clinton attributed his recent hospitalization to his super busy schedule and his lack of sleep.

God is a jealous God. In the Old Testament, He was replaced by a golden calf. Nowadays, He's being bumped by technology and our growing dependence on it. On the plus side, technology has helped with progress in medicine and many other fields. It makes chores more efficient and keeps families connected across the miles with the Internet. But, if you want to be in touch with God, be sure to make the time to unplug your gadgets and make time for Him. Depend on Him not just technology.

Making Time for God

Our days and evenings are filled with school, work, taking our kids to school, soccer practice, music lessons, errands, grocery shopping, doctor appointments, cooking, and cleaning. Everyone's calendar is chock full and filled with stuff to do. There are so many things to do, so little time it seems, to get them done. How can we give God His time? Making extra time for God may seem challenging or nearly impossible but make Him your priority and the rest will fall into place. If you are pressed for time, try waking up an hour earlier and commune with Him before getting the kids off to school or getting ready for work. Ask Him to guide your day and decisions.

Or, if you truly hate rising early, cut your lunch hour in half. Use thirty minutes for your lunch and the last half of the hour in quiet meditation and prayer. You'll be amazed how different your work environment will begin to feel. Several friends and I tried this a few years ago and were amazed at the serenity that entered our office and followed us home. Another time finder I implemented was cutting my television and computer use down. When Pope John Paul II suggested one year, that people turn off the NFL during Lent, I knew he was referring to people like me. I understood his point but I wasn't strong enough to follow his suggestion for Lent. I was addicted to Sunday games and was no better than a heroin addict. I knew that too. It took me a few years but I have finally gotten to the point where I am able to put God before the television shows and computer on any given day, not just any given Sunday. I stopped my NFL addiction cold turkey. I had to get my priorities straight.

There is an old Pennsylvania Dutch saying, 'The faster I go, the behinder I get.' Does that sound like you? Are you playing beat the clock? If so, decide to change now. Do you commute to work via public transit? Next time you hop on your commuter train, unplug your earphones, and plug into some private prayer time. Only you and He know your daily schedule.

Review it and discover hidden pockets of time to get in touch with God. When you do, He'll be in touch with you.

Exercise

If you are ready to ditch your alarm clock, ask your Guardian Angel to wake you in the morning. Tell your angel the time to wake you and trust in your invisible friend to come through for you. This method has worked for me all of my life and has never failed.

This exercise is meant for the younger generation, the Wired/Connected Generation. Take a break day from your electronic gadgets. Yes, I realize I am asking you to give up a lot. Try it for one day. Spend an afternoon and connect with nature. Leave your mobile phone at home. There is no way you can be in a nature setting and not feel the Presence of God surrounding you.

This is for those people of a certain age who remember time BC, before computers. Imagine you are back in the days before the internet was invented. You were happy then. Do today what you did back in the day and experience simplicity. Take some unscheduled time and spend it with God, in your thoughts, in your home, in a church, or in nature. Hand Him your stress and embrace an attitude of freedom for the day. Once you start this exercise repeat as needed. Enjoy.

Numbers

Are you aware of certain numbers following you through life? I'm often asked about the significance of numbers and especially the significance of seeing 11:11. I became aware of 11:11 in 1974. I began to see it on my clock on a regular basis. Soon it began to appear in mysterious ways in my life. It would be either the amount I owed at the checkout counter, or it was the amount of change I received. It manifested as addresses where I had to attend meetings, or showed up as the time I had made a purchase, with the time appearing on my store receipt. I have been told by many teachers that 11:11 relates to ascending to a higher Spiritual Vibration. Watch for this number to appear in your life as we approach December 21, 2012.

Seeing 2, or 222, indicates that your ideas are taking shape. Don't get discouraged; persevere with your plans. Cultivate patience because you're about to reap what you have sown.

Seeing 3, or 333, represents the power of The Blessed Trinity with you. This confirms that you are on the right path and will receive spiritual assistance reaching your goals.

Seeing 4, or 444, is the number of the angels. If you see this number on the clock, as you are contemplating a specific question, the angels are answering you in the affirmative. Your answer is a big yes.

Seeing 5, or 555, is an indication that change is coming into your life, whether you are seeking it or not. It will find you. This number surrounded me while I was going through a major change in my life in 2006. It was a change I didn't want to happen. I was hoping to see 4:44 but I never did. Instead, every time I checked the time, it was 5:55. Looking back, the change that came into my life turned out to be for the best. I couldn't see it as I was going through it, but in hindsight, I see the great blessings that were bestowed on me as the change came into my life. Two stern angels came to me regarding this change. I argued my point, stating the case of why I did not want the change, but they didn't give an inch. Finally, I accepted the change and agreed with the angels. I thought the change was going to kill me, but it cured me. I apologize to them almost daily that I was such an idiot four years ago. Now I realize the mega blessings that came to me along with the change. Had I stayed with the status quo I would have missed them. I will never argue with an angel again. Lesson learned. Mea culpa, Francis.

Seeing 6, or 666, denotes that you need to detach from the

material and instead, get in line with the spiritual side of life. Take a break from shopping at the mall, online, or the flea market. Retreat with a spiritual book or two, to bring the much needed balance that is lacking back into your life. Take care of your soul first and the rest will be given unto you. It's Natural Law.

Seeing 7, or 777, means that you are connecting with God. 7 is His number. Keep doing whatever it is that you have been doing, whether meditation, prayer, or volunteering. As you ascend, and your spiritual frequency rises, you'll be called into service to help others.

Seeing 8, or 888, is a sign of prosperity, abundance and security. Share your blessings with others who need a hand up. You're going to be a beacon of hope for them.

Seeing 9, or 999, represents completion. One chapter of your life is coming to an end, and another fresh chapter is about to be written by you. Be fearless.

Other numbers that follow you may be significant messages from the Other Side of Life. I have a friend, whose mother crossed on October 9th. Every October 9th she receives some kind of windfall, whether an unexpected pay raise or winning a trip at work. It always makes her feel that her mother is sending her the message not to cry on this date, but to celebrate her mother's transition to a higher realm.

Exercise

Notice numbers that keep appearing in your life. It may be your address numbers showing up unexpectedly, your new phone number, your work address, or even your bank balance. Numbers hold meaningful messages for you. Once you become aware of the digits in your life and what they are saying, you'll see silent messages for you and unspoken guidance leading you.

Psalms to Solve Problems

People often think I possess Harry Potter's magic wand to wave over their problems. I don't have a magic wand, fairy dust or four leaf clovers to give away. I do have a powerful book which I refer to and read daily. It's called the Bible. I am sure you've heard of it. You may even have one. This book can help you solve your problems. I began to pray the psalms in 1972 when I learned that each psalm answers a specific petition.

The Book of Psalms is a book of praise, pleas for help, and heartfelt thanks. There is a psalm for every situation and problem that you might experience in life. The Bible is full of stories about people going through mega problems. Slavery, hunger, poverty, lack, being tossed into a fiery furnace, or swallowed by a giant whale are just a few challenges that were faced by people in the Old Testament. Here are psalms to assist you in your times of trial today.

Perhaps you once had a close relationship with God but it deteriorated through the years. Or, perhaps you are hoping for someone close to you or someone in your family to return to God and His Family. Psalm 145 is a good place to start with this intention in mind.

Psalm 145: Be Closer with God

Praise the Lord, O my soul. I will praise the Lord with my life. I will sing psalms to my God as long as I shall be. Do not trust in the leaders, in the sons of men, in whom there is no salvation.

His spirit will depart, and he will return to his earth. In that day, all their thoughts will perish.

Blessed is he whose help is the God of Jacob: His hope is in the Lord God himself, who made heaven and earth, the sea, and all the things that are in them.

He preserves the truth forever. He executes judgment for those who suffer injury. He provides food for the hungry. The Lord releases those who are bound.

The Lord enlightens the blind. The Lord sets upright those who have been thrown down. The Lord loves the just. The Lord watches over new arrivals. He will support the orphan and the widow. And He will destroy the ways of sinners. The Lord shall reign forever: your God, O Zion, from generation to generation

Psalm 1: Spiritual Protection

Blessed is the man who has not followed the counsel of the impious, and has not remained in the way of sinners, and has not sat in the chair of pestilence.

But his will is with the law of the Lord, and he will meditate on his law, day and night.

And he will be like a tree that has been planted beside running waters which will provide its fruit in its time, and its leaf will not fall away, and all things whatsoever that he does will prosper.

Not so the impious, not so. They are like the dust that the wind casts along the face of the earth.

Therefore, the impious will not prevail again in judgment nor sinners in the council of the just.

For the Lord knows the way of the just. And the path of the impious will pass away.

Psalm 24: Spiritual Protection

To you, Lord, I have lifted up my soul.

In you, my God, I trust. Let me not be put to shame.

And do not let my enemies laugh at me. For all who remain with you will not be confounded.

May all those who act unjustly over nothing be confounded, O Lord demonstrate your ways to me, and teach me your paths.

Direct me in your truth, and teach me. For you are God, my savior and I will remain with you all day long.

O Lord, remember your compassion and your mercies, which

are from ages past.

Do not remember the offenses of my youth and my ignorances. Remember me according to your mercy, because of your goodness, O Lord.

The Lord is sweet and righteous. Because of this, He will grant a law to those who fall short in the way.

He will direct the mild in judgment. He will teach the meek his ways.

All the ways of the Lord are mercy and truth, to those who yearn for his covenant and his testimonies.

Because of your name, O Lord, you will pardon my sin, for it is great.

Which is the man who fears the Lord? He has established a law for him, on the way that he has chosen.

His soul will dwell upon good things, and his offspring will inherit the earth.

The Lord is a firmament to those who fear Him, and His covenant will be made manifest to them.

My eyes are ever toward the Lord, for he will pull my feet from the snare. Look upon me and have mercy on me; for I am alone and poor.

The troubles of my heart have been multiplied. Deliver me from my needfulness. See my lowliness and my hardship, and release all my offenses.

Consider my enemies, for they have been multiplied, and they have hated me with an unjust hatred.

Preserve my soul and rescue me. I will not be ashamed, for I have hoped in You.

The innocent and the righteous have adhered to me, because I have remained with You.

Free Israel, O God, from all his tribulations.

Psalm 77: Strengthen Your Faith

O my people attend to my law. Incline your ears to the words of my mouth.

I will open my mouth in parables. I will speak about concepts that are from the beginning.

We have heard and known such great things, as our fathers have described to us.

These things have not been hidden from their sons in any generation: Declaring the praises of the Lord, and His virtues, and the wonders that He has done.

And He has received testimony with Jacob, and He has set a law within Israel. Such great things, He has commanded our fathers, so as to make these things known to their sons.

So that another generation might know them, and so that the sons, who will be born and who will grow up, shall describe them to their sons.

So then, may they put their hope in God, and may they not forget the works of God, and may they seek His commandments.

May they not become like their fathers, a perverse and exasperating generation: A generation that does not straighten their heart and whose spirit is not trustworthy with God.

The sons of Ephraim, who bend and shoot the bow, have been turned back in the day of battle.

They have not kept the covenant of God. And they were not willing to walk in His law.

And they have been forgetful of His benefits, and of His miracles, which He revealed to them.

He performed miracles in the sight of their fathers, in the land of Egypt, in the field of Tanis.

He broke the sea and He led them through. And He stationed the waters, as if in a vessel.

And He led them with a cloud by day and with illumination by fire throughout the night.

He broke through the rock in the wasteland, and He gave them to drink, as if from the great abyss.

He brought forth water from the rock, and He conducted the

waters, as if they were rivers.

And yet, they continued to sin against Him. In a waterless place, they provoked the Most High with resentment.

And they tempted God in their hearts, by asking for food according to their desires.

And they spoke badly about God. They said, 'Would God be able to prepare a table in the desert?'

He struck the rock, and so waters flowed and the torrents flooded, but would even he be able to provide bread, or provide a table, for his people?'

Therefore, the Lord heard, and He was dismayed, and a fire was kindled within Jacob and anger ascended into Israel.

For they neither put their trust in God, nor did they hope in His salvation.

And He commanded the clouds from above, and He opened the doors of heaven.

And He rained down manna upon them to eat, and He gave them the bread of heaven.

Man ate the bread of Angels. He sent them provisions in abundance.

He transferred the south wind from heaven, and, in His virtue, He brought in the Southwest wind.

And He rained down flesh upon them, as if it were dust, and feathered birds, as if they were the sand of the sea.

And they fell down in the midst of their camp, encircling their tabernacles.

And they ate until they were greatly satisfied, and He brought to them according to their desires.

They were not cheated out of what they wanted. Their food was still in their mouth, and then the wrath of God came upon them.

And He slew the fat ones among them, and He impeded the elect of Israel.

In all these things, they continued to sin, and they were not trustworthy with His miracles.

And their days faded away into vanity, and their years with haste.

When He slew them, then they sought Him. And they returned, and they drew near to Him in the early morning. And they were mindful that God is their helper and that the Most High God is their redeemer.

And they chose Him with their mouth, and then they lied to Him with their tongue.

Their hearts were not upright with Him nor have they been living faithfully in His covenant.

Yet He is merciful, and He will pardon their sins. And He will not destroy them.

And He has abundantly turned aside His own wrath. And He did not enflame His wrath entirely.

And He remembered that they are flesh: With a spirit that goes forth and does not return.

How often did they provoke Him in the desert and stir Him to wrath in a waterless place?

And they turned back and tempted God, and they exasperated the Holy One of Israel.

They did not remember His Hand, in the day that He redeemed them from the hand of the one troubling them.

Thus, He positioned His signs in Egypt and His wonders in the field of Tanis.

And He turned their rivers into blood, along with their rain showers, so that they could not drink.

He sent among them the common fly, and it devoured them, and the frog, and it scattered them.

And He gave up their fruits to mold and their labors to the locust.

And He slew their vineyards with hail and their mulberry trees with severe frost.

And He delivered their cattle to the hail and their possessions to fire.

And He sent the wrath of His indignation among them: Indignation and wrath and tribulation, sent forth by evil angels.

He made way for the path of His anger. He did not spare their souls from death. And He enclosed their beasts of burden in death.

And He struck all the first-born in the land of Egypt: the first fruits of all their labor in the tabernacles of Ham.

And He took away His own people like sheep, and He led them through the wilderness like a flock.

And He led them out in hope, and they did not fear. And the sea covered their enemies.

And He led them to the mountain of His sanctification: the mountain that His right Hand had acquired. And He cast out the Gentiles before their face. And He divided their land by lot to them, with a line of distribution.

And He caused the tribes of Israel to dwell in their tabernacles.

Yet they tempted and aggravated God Most High, and they did not keep His testaments.

And they turned themselves aside, and they did not serve the covenant.

In the same manner as their fathers, they were turned backwards, like a crooked bow.

They impelled Him to anger on their hills, and they provoked Him to rivalry with their graven images.

God listened, and He spurned them, and He reduced Israel greatly, almost to nothing.

And He rejected the tabernacle of Shiloh, His tabernacle where He had dwelt among men.

And He delivered their virtue into captivity, and their beauty into the hands of the enemy.

And He enclosed his people with the sword, and He spurned his inheritance.

Fire consumed their young men, and their virgins were not lamented.

Their priests fell by the sword, and their widows did not weep.

And the Lord was awaked, as if out of sleep, and like a powerful man impaired by wine.

And He struck His enemies on the back. He gave them over to everlasting disgrace.

And He rejected the tabernacle of Joseph, and He did not choose the tribe of Ephraim.

But He chose the tribe of Judah: Mount Zion, which he loved.

And He built up His sanctuary, like a single-horned beast, in the land that He founded for all ages.

And He chose His servant David, and He took him from the flocks of the sheep:

He received him from following the ewes with their young, in order to pasture Jacob His servant and Israel His inheritance.

And He fed them with the innocence of His heart. And He led them with the understanding of His Hands.

The one question I receive more than any other is, 'What is my purpose in life? What should I be doing?' I believe that we know in childhood, exactly what we would like to be when we grow up. I knew at age nine that I wanted to write. If you can't name your passion (I have met women in their 50s who have no idea what they want to do in life), pray Psalm 149. God will guide you. He may show you in a dream. He may toss hints at you that you just can't miss, or He may bring many coincidences into your life to make His point crystal clear to you. He will show up with your answer if you trust Him.

Psalm 149: Know Your Purpose in Life
Alleluia. Sing to the Lord a new song. His praise is in the Church of the saints.

Let Israel rejoice in Him who made them, and let the sons of Zion exult in their king.

Let them praise His Name in chorus. Let them sing psalms to Him with the timbrel and the psaltery.

The Lord is well pleased with His people, and He will exalt the meek unto salvation.

The saints will exult in glory. They will rejoice upon their couches.

The exultations of God will be in their throat, and two-edged swords will be in their hands:

To obtain vindication among the nations, chastisements among the peoples, bind their kings, with shackles, and their nobles with manacles of iron, to obtain judgment over them, as it has been written.

This is glory for all his saints. Alleluia.

Psalm 143: Increase Hope

Blessed is the Lord, my God, who trains my hands for the battle and my fingers for the war.

My mercy and my refuge, my supporter and my deliverer, my protector and Him in whom I have hoped: He subdues my people under me.

O Lord, what is man that you have become known to him? Or the son of man, that You consider him? Man has been made similar to vanity. His days pass by like a shadow.

O Lord, incline Your heavens and descend. Touch the mountains, and they will smoke.

Send a flash of lightning, and You will scatter them. Shoot Your arrows, and You will set them in disarray.

Send forth Your Hand from on high: Rescue me, and free me from many waters, from the hand of the sons of foreigners.

Their mouth has been speaking vain things, and their right hand is the right hand of iniquity.

To you, O God, I will sing a new song. On the psaltery, with an instrument of ten strings, I will sing psalms to You.

He gives salvation to kings. He has redeemed your servant David from the malignant sword.

Rescue me, and deliver me from the hand of the sons of foreigners.

Their mouth has been speaking vain things, and their right hand is the right hand of iniquity.

Their sons are like new plantings in their youth. Their daughters are dressed up: Adorned all around like the idols of a temple.

Their cupboards are full: Overflowing from one thing into another. Their sheep bear young, brought forth in abundance.

Their cattle are fat. There is no ruined wall or passage, nor anyone crying out in their streets.

They have called the people that have these things: blessed. But blessed is the people whose God is the Lord.

Psalm 137: Overcoming Temptation

O Lord, I will confess to You with my whole heart, for You have heard the words of my mouth. I will sing psalms to You in the sight of the Angels.

I will adore before Your holy temple, and I will confess Your Name: It is above Your mercy and Your truth. You have magnified Your holy Name above all.

On whatever day that I will call upon You: Hear me. You will multiply virtue in my soul.

May all the kings of the earth confess to You O Lord for they have heard all the words of Your mouth.

And let them sing in accordance with the ways of the Lord.

For great is the glory of the Lord.

The Lord is exalted, and He looks with favor on the humble. But the lofty He knows from a distance.

If I wander into the midst of tribulation, You will revive me. For You extended Your Hand against the wrath of my enemies. And Your right Hand has accomplished my salvation.

The Lord will provide retribution on my behalf. O Lord, Your mercy is forever. Do not disdain the works of Your Hands

Psalm 5: Business Success

The world is experiencing a recession affecting millions of people around the world. This psalm is prayed to change lack into abundance.

O Lord, listen closely to my words. Understand my outcry. Attend to the voice of my prayer, my King and my God. For to You, I will pray. In the morning, Lord, you will hear my voice. In the morning, I will stand before You, and I will see.

For You are not a God who wills iniquity. And the malicious will not dwell close to You, nor will the unjust endure before Your Eyes.

You hate all who work iniquity. You will destroy all who speak a lie. The bloody and deceitful man, the Lord will abominate.

But I am in the multitude of Your mercy. I will enter Your house. I will show adoration toward Your holy temple, in Your fear.

Lord, lead me in Your justice. Because of my enemies, direct my way in Your sight.

For there is no truth in their mouth: Their heart is vain. Their throat is an open sepulcher. They have acted deceitfully with their tongues.

Judge them, O God. Let them fall by their own intentions: According to the multitude of their impiety, expel them. For they have provoked You, O Lord.

But let all those who hope in You rejoice. They will exult in eternity, and You will dwell in them. And all those who love Your Name will glory in You.

For You will bless the just. You have crowned us, O Lord, as if with a shield of Your Good Will.

Have you been at your job for some time now, yet are looked over at promotion time? Praying Psalm 75 might be the answer to your prayer for promotion.

Psalm 75: Career Advancement

In Judea, God is known. In Israel, His Name is great. And His place has been formed with peace. And His dwelling place is in Zion.

In that place, He has broken the powers of the bows, the shield, the sword, and the battle.

You illuminate wondrously from the mountains of eternity. All the foolish of heart have been disturbed. They have slept their sleep, and all the men of riches have found nothing in their hands.

At Your rebuke, O God of Jacob, those who were mounted on horseback have fallen asleep.

You are terrible, and so, who can withstand You? From thence is your wrath.

You have caused judgment to be heard from heaven. The earth trembled and was quieted, when God rose up in judgment in order to bring salvation to all the meek of the earth.

The thinking of man will confess to You, and the legacy of his thinking will keep a feast day to You.

Make vows and pay them to the Lord, your God. All you who surround Him bring gifts: To Him Who is terrible, even to Him who takes away the spirit of leaders, to Him Who is terrible with the kings of the earth.

Psalm 35: Have a Special Prayer Answered

The unjust one has said within himself that he would commit offenses. There is no fear of God before his eyes.

He has acted deceitfully in His sight, such that his iniquity will be found to be hatred.

The words of his mouth are iniquity and deceit. He is unwilling to understand, so that he may act well.

He has been considering iniquity on his bed. He has set himself on every way that is not good; moreover, he has not hated evil.

Lord, Your mercy is in heaven, and Your truth is even to the clouds.

Your justice is like the mountains of God. Your judgments are a great abyss. Men and beasts, You will save, O Lord.

How You have multiplied Your mercy, O God. And so the sons of men will hope under the cover of Your Wings.

They will be inebriated with the fruitfulness of Your house, and You will give them to drink from the torrent of Your enjoyment.

For with You is the fountain of life; and within Your Light, we will see the Light.

Extend Your mercy before those who know You and Your justice to these, who are upright in heart.

May arrogant feet not approach me, and may the hand of the sinner not disturb me.

In that place, those who work iniquity have fallen. They have been expelled; they were not able to stand.

Psalm 32: Emotional Strength

The Lord has reigned. He has been clothed with beauty.

The Lord has been clothed with strength, and He has girded Himself.

Yet He has also confirmed the world, which will not be moved.

My throne is prepared from of old. You are from everlasting.

The floods have lifted up, O Lord the floods have lifted up their voice.

The floods have lifted up their waves, before the noise of many waters.

Wondrous are the surges of the sea; wondrous is the Lord on high.

Your testimonies have been made exceedingly trustworthy.

Sanctity befits your house, O Lord, with length of days.

Psalm 42 Emotional Healing

Judge me, O God, and discern my cause from that of a nation not holy; rescue me from a man unjust and deceitful.

For You are God my strength. Why have You rejected me?

And why do I walk in sadness, while the adversary afflicts me?

Send forth Your Light and Your truth. They have guided me and led me, to Your holy mountain and into Your tabernacles. And I will enter, up to the altar of God, to God who enlivens my youthfulness.

To you, O God, my God, I will confess upon a stringed instrument.

Why are you sad, my soul? And why do you disquiet me?

Hope in God, for I will still give praise to Him: the salvation of my countenance and my God.

Psalm 82: Release Fear

There are two powers on this planet, the power of fear and the power of love. When you feed on fear you are embracing defeat.

When you let go of fear, refuse to embrace it, and heed the Words of Jesus, 'Fear not' you will see amazing results manifest in your life.

O God, who will ever be like You? Do not be silent, and do not be unmoved, O God.

For behold, Your enemies have sounded off, and those who hate You have carried out a head.

They have acted with malice in counsel over Your people, and they have plotted against Your holy ones.

They have said, 'Come, let us scatter them from the nations

and not allow the name of Israel to be remembered any longer.'

For they plotted unanimously joined together against You, they ordained a covenant:

The tabernacle of Edomites and Ishmaelites, and Moab and the Hagarites, and Gebal, and Ammon, and Amalek, the foreigners among the inhabitants of Tyre.

For even Assur comes with them. They have become the helpers of the sons of Lot.

Do to them as You did to Midian and Sisera, just as to Jabin at the torrent of Kishon.

They perished at Endor, and they became like the dung of the earth.

Set their leaders to be like Oreb and Zeeb, and Zebah and Zalmunna: all their leaders who said, 'Let us possess the Sanctuary of God for an inheritance.'

My God, set them like a wheel, and like stubble before the face of the wind.

Set them like a fire burning up the forest, and like a flame burning up the mountains.

So will You pursue them in Your tempest, and disturb them in your wrath.

Fill their faces with shame, and they will seek Your Name, O Lord.

Let them be ashamed and troubled, from age to age, and let them be confounded and perish.

And let them know that the Lord is Your Name. You alone are the Most High in all the earth.

To Restore Relationships

There are different kinds of healing. There are prayers for Financial Healing, Physical Healing, Emotional Healing, and Relationship Healing, to name several. Psalm 45 is prayed by a man who wishes to restore his marriage.

Psalm 45

Our God is our refuge and strength, a helper in the tribulations that have greatly overwhelmed us.

Because of this, we will not be afraid when the earth will be turbulent and the mountains will be transferred into the heart of the sea.

They thundered, and the waters were stirred up among them; the mountains have been disturbed by His strength.

The frenzy of the river rejoices the city of God. The Most High has sanctified His tabernacle.

God is in its midst: It will not be shaken. God will assist it in the early morning.

The peoples have been disturbed, and the kingdoms have been bowed down. He uttered his voice: The earth has been moved.

The Lord of hosts is with us. The God of Jacob is our supporter.

Draw near and behold the works of the Lord: what portents He has set upon the earth, carrying away wars even to the end of the earth.

He will crush the bow and break the weapons, and He will burn the shield with fire.

Be empty, and see that I am God. I will be exalted among the peoples, and I will be exalted upon the earth.

The Lord of hosts is with us. The God of Jacob is our supporter.

Psalm 46 is prayed by a woman who wishes to restore her marriage.

Psalm 46

All nations, clap your hands. Shout joyfully to God with a voice of exultation.

For the Lord is exalted and terrible: A great King over all the earth.

He has subjected the peoples to us and subdued the nations under our feet.

He has chosen us for his inheritance: The splendor of Jacob, whom He has loved.

God ascends with jubilation, and the Lord with the voice of the trumpet.

Sing psalms to our God, sing psalms. Sing psalms to our King, sing psalms.

For God is the King of all the earth. Sing psalms wisely.

God will reign over the peoples. God sits upon his holy throne.

The leaders of the peoples have been gathered together by the God of Abraham.

Psalm 147: Brings Serenity to the Home

Alleluia. Praise the Lord, O Jerusalem. Praise your God, O Zion.

He has reinforced the bars of your gates. He has blessed your sons within you.

He has stationed peace at your borders, and He has satisfied you with the fat of the grain.

He sends forth his eloquence to the earth. His word runs swiftly.

He provides snow like wool. He strews clouds like ashes.

He sends his ice crystals like morsels. Who can stand firm before the face of His cold?

He will send forth His Word, and it will melt them. His Spirit will breathe out, and the waters will flow.

He announces His Word to Jacob, His justices and His judgments to Israel.

He has not done so much for every nation, and He has not made His judgments manifest to them. Alleluia.

Psalm 44: Receive God's Guidance in Your Dreams

My heart has uttered a good word. I speak of my works to the king. My tongue is like the pen of a scribe who writes quickly.

You are a brilliant form before the sons of men. Grace has been poured freely into your lips. Because of this, God has blessed you in eternity.

Fasten your sword to your thigh, O most powerful one.

With your splendor and your excellence extended, proceed prosperously and reign for the sake of truth and meekness and justice, and so will your right hand lead you wondrously.

Your arrows are sharp; the people will fall under you, with the hearts of the enemies of the king.

Your throne, O God, is forever and ever. The scepter of Your kingdom is a scepter of true aim.

You have loved justice and hated iniquity. Because of this, God, your God, has anointed you, before your co-heirs, with the oil of gladness.

Myrrh and balsam and cinnamon perfume your garments, from the houses of ivory. From these, they have delighted you: The daughters of kings in your honor.

The queen assisted at your right hand, in clothing of gold, encircled with diversity.

Listen, daughter, and see, and incline your ear. And forget your people and your father's house.

And the king will desire your beauty. For he is the Lord your God, and they will adore Him.

And the daughters of Tyre will entreat your countenance with gifts: All the rich men of the people.

All the glory of the daughter of its king is inside, in golden fringes clothed all around with diversities. After her, virgins will be led to the king.

Her neighbors will be brought to you. They will be brought with gladness and exultation. They will be led into the temple of the king.

For your fathers, sons have been born to you. You will establish them as leaders over all the earth.

They will remember Your Name always, for generation after generation. Because of this, people will confess to You in eternity, even forever and ever

Psalm 50: Open Your Spiritual Eyes

Be merciful to me, O God, according to Your great Mercy.

And, according to the plentitude of Your Compassion, wipe out my iniquity.

Wash me once again from my iniquity, and cleanse me from my sin.

I know my iniquity, and my sin is ever before me. Against You only have I sinned, and I have done evil before Your Eyes.

And so, You are justified in Your Words, and You will prevail when You give judgment.

For behold, I was conceived in iniquities, and in sinfulness did my mother conceive me.

For behold, You have loved truth. The obscure and hidden things of Your Wisdom, You have manifested to me.

You will sprinkle me with hyssop, and I will be cleansed. You will wash me, and I will be made whiter than snow.

In my hearing, You will grant gladness and rejoicing. And the bones that have been humbled will exult.

Turn Your Face away from my sins, and erase all my iniquities.

Create a clean heart in me, O God. And renew an upright spirit within my inmost being.

Do not cast me away from Your Face; and do not take your Holy Spirit from me.

Restore to me the joy of Your Salvation, and confirm me with an unsurpassed spirit.

I will teach the unjust Your Ways, and the impious will be converted to you.

Free me from blood, O God, the God of my salvation, and my

tongue will extol Your Justice.

O Lord, You will open my lips, and my mouth will announce Your Praise.

If You had desired sacrifice, I would certainly have given it, but with holocausts, You will not be delighted.

A crushed spirit is a sacrifice to God. A contrite and humbled heart, O God, You will not spurn.

Act kindly, Lord, in Your Good Will toward Zion, so that the walls of Jerusalem may be built up.

Then You will accept the sacrifice of justice, oblations, and holocausts. Then they will lay calves upon Your Altar.

Psalm 49: Activate and Increase Clairvoyance

The God of gods, the Lord has spoken, and He has called the earth, from the rising of the sun even to its setting, from Zion, the brilliance of His Beauty.

God will arrive manifestly. Our God also will not keep silence. A fire will flare up in His Sight, and a mighty tempest will surround Him.

He will call to heaven from above, and to the earth, to discern his people.

Gather His holy ones to Him, you who order His covenant above sacrifices.

And the heavens will announce His Justice. For God is the Judge.

Listen, my people, and I will speak. Listen, Israel, and I will testify for you. I am God, your God.

I will not reprove you for your sacrifices. Moreover, your holocausts are ever in My Sight.

I will not accept calves from your house nor he goats from your flocks.

For all the wild beasts of the forest are Mine: The cattle on the hills and the oxen.

I know all the flying things of the air, and the beauty of the field is with Me.

If I should be hungry, I would not tell you: For the whole world is Mine and all its plentitude.

Shall I gnaw on the flesh of bulls? Or would I drink the blood of oats?

Offer to God the sacrifice of praise, and pay your vows to the Most High.

And call upon Me in the day of tribulation. I will rescue you, and you will honor Me.

But to the sinner, God has said: Why do you discourse on My justices, and take up My covenant through your mouth?

Truly, you have hated discipline, and you have cast My sermons behind you.

If you saw a thief, you ran with him, and you have placed your portion with adulterers.

Your mouth has abounded with malice, and your tongue has concocted deceits.

Sitting, you spoke against your brother, and you set up a scandal against your mother's son.

These things you have done, and I was silent. You thought, unjustly, that I ought to be like you.

But I will reprove you, and I will set myself against your face.

Understand these things, you who forget God; lest at any time, He might quickly take you away, and there would be no one to rescue you.

The sacrifice of praise will honor me. And in that place is the journey by which I will reveal to him the salvation of God

Psalm 61: Find Your Right Home

Will my soul not be subject to God? For from Him is my salvation.

Yes, He Himself is my God and my salvation. He is my supporter; I will be moved no more.

How is it that you rush against a man? Every one of you puts to death, as if you were pulling down a ruined wall, leaning over and falling apart.

So, truly, they intended to reject my price. I ran in thirst. They blessed with their mouth and cursed with their heart. Yet, truly, my soul will be subject to God. For from Him is my patience.

He is my God and my Savior. He is my helper; I will not be expelled.

In God is my salvation and my glory. He is the God of my help, and my hope is in God.

All peoples gathered together: Trust in Him. Pour out your hearts in His Sight. God is our helper for eternity.

So, truly, the sons of men are untrustworthy. The sons of men are liars in the scales, so that, by emptiness, they may deceive among themselves.

Do not trust in iniquity, and do not desire plunder. If riches flow toward you, do not be willing to set your heart on them. God has spoken once. I have heard two things: That power belongs to God, and that mercy belongs to You, O Lord. For you will repay each one according to his works.

Psalm 84: Be Optimistic When Tested

O Lord, You have blessed Your Land. You have turned aside the captivity of Jacob.

You have released the iniquity of Your people. You have covered all their sins.

You have mitigated all Your Wrath. You have turned aside from the wrath of Your Indignation.

Convert us, O God, our Savior, and turn Your Anger away from us.

Will You be angry with us forever? And will You extend Your Wrath from generation to generation?

O God, You will turn back and revive us. And your people will rejoice in you.

O Lord reveal to us Your Mercy and grant to us Your Salvation.

I will listen to what the Lord God may be saying to me.

He will speak peace to His people, and to His saints, and to those who are being converted to the heart.

So then, truly His Salvation is near to those who fear Him, so that glory may inhabit our land.

Mercy and truth have met each other. Justice and peace have missed.

Truth has risen from the earth, and justice has gazed down from heaven.

For so will the Lord give goodness, and our earth will give her fruit.

Justice will walk before Him, and He will set His steps upon the way

Psalm 85: Mend Broken Friendships

Incline your ear, O Lord, and hear me. I am needy and poor.

Preserve my soul, for I am holy. My God, bring salvation to Your servant who hopes in You.

O Lord, be merciful to me, for I have cried out to You all day long.

Give joy to the soul of your servant, for I have lifted up my soul to You, Lord.

You are sweet and mild Lord and plentiful in mercy to all who call upon You.

Pay attention, Lord, to my prayer, and attend to the voice of my supplication.

In the day of my tribulation, I cried out to You, because You heeded me.

There is no one like You among the gods, O Lord, and there is no one like You in Your works.

All the nations, which You have made, will draw near and adore in Your presence, O Lord. And they will glorify Your

Name.

You are great, and You perform wonders. You alone are God.

Lead me, O Lord, in your way, and I will walk in Your Truth.

May my heart rejoice, so I will fear Your Name.

I will confess to You, O Lord my God, with my whole heart.

And I will glorify Your Name in eternity.

Your Mercy toward me is great, and You have rescued my soul from the lower part of hell.

O God, the iniquitous have risen up against me, the synagogue of the powerful, have sought my soul, and they have not placed You in their sight.

And you, Lord God, are compassionate and merciful, being patient and full of mercy and truthful.

Look down upon me and have mercy on me. Grant Your Authority to Your servant, and bring salvation to the son of your handmaid.

Make me a sign of what is good, so that those who hate me may look and be confounded.

For you, O Lord, have helped me and consoled me

Psalm 88: Heal an Argument

I will sing the mercies of the Lord in eternity. I will announce Your Truth with my mouth, from generation to generation.

You have said: Mercy will be built in the heavens, unto eternity. Your truth will be prepared there.

I have set up a covenant with My elect. I have sworn to David My servant:

I will prepare your offspring, even in eternity. And I will build up your throne, from generation to generation.

The heavens will confess Your miracles, Lord, and also Your truth, in the church of the saints.

For who among the clouds is equal to the Lord? Who among the sons of God is like God?

God is glorified by the counsel of the saints. He is great and terrible above all those who are around Him.

O Lord, God of hosts, who is like you? You are powerful, Lord, and Your truth is all around You.

You rule over the power of the sea, and You even mitigate the movement of its waves.

You have humbled the arrogant one, like one who has been wounded. You have scattered Your enemies with the Arm of Your strength.

Yours are the heavens, and Yours is the earth. You founded the whole world in all its fullness.

You created the north and the sea. Tabor and Hermon will exult in Your Name.

Your Arm acts with power. Let Your Hand be strengthened, and let Your Right Hand be exalted.

Justice and judgment are the preparation of Your Throne. Mercy and truth will precede Your Face.

Blessed are the people that know jubilation. They will walk in the Light of Your Countenance, O Lord, and they will exult in Your Name all day long, and they will be exalted in Your justice.

For You are the glory of their virtue, and in Your Goodness, our horn will be exalted.

Our assumption is of the Lord, and it is of our King, the Holy One of Israel.

Then You spoke in a vision to Your holy ones, and You said: I have stationed help with the powerful one, and I have exalted the elect one from my people.

I have found my servant David. I have anointed him with my holy oil.

My Hand will assist him, and My Arm will fortify him. The enemy will have no advantage over him, nor will the son of iniquity be positioned to harm him.

And I will cut down his enemies before his face. And those who hate him, I will turn to flight.

And My Truth and My Mercy will be with him. And his horn

will be exalted in My Name.

And I will place his hand on the sea and his right hand on the rivers.

He will invoke Me: 'You are my Father, my God, and the support of my salvation.'

And I will make him the first-born, preeminent before the kings of the earth.

I will preserve My Mercy for him eternally and My covenant for him faithfully.

And I will set his offspring from generation to generation, and his throne like the days of heaven.

But if his sons abandon My law, and if they do not walk in My judgments, if they profane My justices, and if they do not keep My Commandments:

I will visit their iniquities with a rod, and their sins with a beating.

But I will not scatter My mercy from him, and I will not do harm to My truth.

And I will not profane My covenant, and I will not make void that which proceeds from My Lips.

I have sworn by My Holiness one time: I will not lie to David his offspring will remain for eternity.

And his throne will be like the sun in My Sight, and, like the moon, it is perfected in eternity, and it is a faithful witness in heaven.

Yet, truly, you have rejected and despised, you have pushed away, My Christ.

You have overthrown the covenant of your servant. You have profaned his sanctuary on earth.

You have destroyed all his fences. You have made his territory dreadful.

All who pass by the way have plundered him. He has become a disgrace to his neighbors.

You have exalted the right hand of those who oppress him.

You have brought joy to all his enemies.

You have diverted the help of his sword, and you have not assisted him in battle.

You have torn him away from cleansing, and you have smashed his throne down to the ground.

You have reduced the days of his time. You have flooded him with confusion.

How long, O Lord will you turn away unto the end? Will Your wrath flare up like a fire?

Remember what my substance is. For could you really have appointed all the sons of men in vain?

Who is the man that will live, and yet not see death? Who will rescue his own soul from the hand of the underworld?

O Lord, where are Your Mercies of antiquity, just as You swore to David in Your Truth?

Be mindful, O Lord, of the disgrace of Your servants which I have sustained in my sinews among many nations.

With these, your enemies have reproached you, O Lord; with these, they have reproached the commutation of your Christ. Blessed is the Lord for all eternity. Amen. Amen

Psalm 92: A Psalm of Gratitude

The Lord has reigned. He has been clothed with beauty. The Lord has been clothed with strength, and He has girded Himself.

Yet He has also confirmed the world, which will not be moved.

My throne is prepared from of old. You are from everlasting. The floods have lifted up, O Lord the floods have lifted up their voice.

The floods have lifted up their waves, before the noise of many waters.

Wondrous are the surges of the sea; wondrous is the Lord on high.

Your testimonies have been made exceedingly trustworthy.

Sanctity befits your house, O Lord, with length of days.

Psalm 105: Forgive and Forget Past Hurts

Alleluia. Confess to the Lord, for He is good, for His mercy is with every generation.

Who will declare the powers of the Lord? Who makes a hearing for all his praises?

Blessed are those who keep judgment and who do justice at all times.

Remember us, O Lord, with Good Will for your people.

Visit us with Your salvation, so that we may see the goodness of Your elect.

So that we may rejoice in the joy of Your nation, so that You may be praised along with Your inheritance.

We have sinned, as have our fathers. We have acted unjustly; we have wrought iniquity.

Our fathers did not understand Your miracles in Egypt. They did not remember the multitude of Your mercies.

And they provoked You, while going up to the sea, even the Red Sea.

And He saved them for the sake of His Name, so that He might make known His Power.

And He rebuked the Red Sea, and it dried up. And He led them into the abyss, as if into a desert.

And He saved them from the hand of those who hated them.

And He redeemed them from the hand of the enemy.

And the water covered those who troubled them. Not one of them remained.

And they believed His Words, and they sang His Praises.

As soon as they had finished, they forgot His works, and they would not endure His counsel.

And they coveted their desire in the desert, and they tempted God in a waterless place.

And He granted to them their request, and He sent abundance into their souls.

And they provoked Moses in the camp, and Aaron, the holy one of the Lord.

The earth opened and swallowed Dathan, and it covered the congregation of Abraham.

And a fire broke out in their congregation. A flame burned up the sinners.

And they fashioned a calf at Horeb, and they adored a graven image.

And they exchanged their glory for the likeness of a calf that eats hay.

They forgot God, Who saved them, Who did great things in Egypt: miracles in the land of Ham, terrible things at the Red Sea.

And He said that He would destroy them, yet Moses, His elect, stood firm before Him in the breach, in order to avert His wrath, lest He destroy them.

And they held the desirable land to be nothing. They did not trust in His Word.

And they murmured in their tabernacles. They did not heed the Voice of the Lord.

And He lifted up His Hand over them, in order to prostrate them in the desert, in order to cast their offspring among the nations, and to scatter them among the regions.

And they were initiated into Baal of Peor, and they ate the sacrifices of the dead.

And they provoked Him with their inventions, and ruination was multiplied in them.

Then Phinehas stood up and placated Him: And so the violent disturbance ceased.

And it was reputed to Him unto justice, from generation to generation, even forever.

And they provoked Him at the Waters of Contradiction, and

Moses was afflicted because of them, for they exasperated his spirit.

And so He divided them with His Lips.

They did not destroy the nations, about which the Lord had spoken to them.

And they were mixed among the Gentiles. And they learned their works, and they served their graven images, and it became a scandal to them.

And they sacrificed their sons and their daughters to demons.

And they shed innocent blood: The blood of their sons and of their daughters, which they sacrificed to the graven images of Canaan.

And the land was infected with bloodshed and was contaminated with their works. And they fornicated according to their own inventions.

And the Lord became furiously angry with His people, and He abhorred His Inheritance.

And He delivered them into the hands of the nations. And those who hated them became rulers over them.

And their enemies afflicted them, and they were humbled under their hands.

Many times, He delivered them. Yet they provoked Him with their counsel, and they were brought low by their iniquities.

And He saw that they were in tribulation, and He heard their prayer.

And He was mindful of His covenant, and He repented according to the multitude of His mercies.

And He provided for them with mercies, in the sight of all those who had seized them.

Save us, O Lord our God, and gather us from the nations, so that we may confess Your Holy Name and glory in Your Praise. Blessed is the Lord God of Israel, from ages past, even to all ages. And let all the people say: Amen. Amen.

Psalm 111: Find Your Right Career

Blessed is the man who fears the Lord. He will prefer His Commandments exceedingly.

His offspring will be powerful on the earth. The generation of the upright will be blessed.

Glory and wealth will be in his house, and his justice shall remain from age to age.

For the upright, a light has risen up in the darkness. He is merciful and compassionate and just.

Pleasing is the man who shows mercy and lends. He will order his words with judgment.

He will not be disturbed in eternity. The just one will be an everlasting memorial.

He will not fear a report of disasters. His heart is prepared to hope in the Lord.

His heart has been confirmed. He will not be disturbed, until he looks down upon his enemies.

He has distributed, he has given to the poor. His justice shall remain from age to age. His horn shall be exalted in glory.

The sinner will see and become angry. He will gnash his teeth and waste away. The desire of sinners will perish.

Psalm 91: Protection

It is good to confess to the Lord and to sing psalms to Your Name, O Most High:

To announce Your mercy in the morning and Your truth throughout the night, upon the ten strings, upon the psaltery, with a canticle, upon stringed instruments.

For you, O Lord, have delighted me with Your doings, and I will exult in the works of Your Hands.

How great are your works, O Lord! Your thoughts have been made exceedingly deep.

A foolish man will not know these things, and a senseless one will not understand:

When sinners will have risen up like grass, and when all those who work iniquity will have appeared, that they shall pass away, age after age.

But you, O Lord, are the Most High for all eternity.

For behold Your enemies, O Lord, for behold Your enemies will perish, and all those who work iniquity will be dispersed.

And my horn will be exalted like that of the single-horned beast, and my old age will be exalted in fruitful mercy.

And my eye has looked down upon my enemies, and my ear will hear of the malignant rising up against me.

The just one will flourish like the palm tree. He will be multiplied like the cedar of Lebanon.

Those planted in the house of the Lord will flourish in the courts of the house of our God.

They will still be multiplied in a fruitful old age, and they will endure well, so that they may announce that the Lord our God is righteous and that there is no iniquity in him.

Psalm 72: Prosperity

How good is God to Israel, to those who are upright in heart. But my feet were nearly moved; my steps had nearly slipped. I was zealous over the iniquitous, seeing the peacefulness of sinners.

They have no respect for their death, nor do they have support in their wounds.

They are not with the hardships of men, nor will they be scourged with men.

Therefore, arrogance has held on to them. They have been covered with their iniquity and impiety.

Their iniquity has proceeded, as if from fat. They have parted from the affection of the heart.

They have thought and spoken wickedness. They have spoken iniquity in high places.

They have set their mouth against heaven, and their tongue has traversed the earth.

Therefore, my people will be converted here, and fullness of days will be found in them.

And they said, 'How would God know?' and, 'Isn't there knowledge in high places?'

Behold, these are sinners, and, abounding in this age, they have obtained riches.

And I said: So then, it is without purpose that I have justified my heart and washed my hands among the innocent.

And I have been scourged all day long, and I have received my chastisement in the mornings.

If I were to say that I would explain this: Behold, I would condemn this nation of your sons.

I considered, so that I might know this. It is a hardship before me until I may enter into the Sanctuary of God, and understand it to its last part.

So, because of deceitfulness, truly, you have placed it before them. While they were being lifted up, you were casting them down.

How have they been brought to desolation? They have suddenly failed. They have perished because of their iniquity.

As a dream is to those who awaken, O Lord, so will You reduce their image to nothing in your city?

My heart has been inflamed, and my temperament has been changed.

And so, I have been reduced to nothing, and I did not know it.

I have become like a beast of burden to You, and I am always with You.

You have held my right hand. And in your will, you have conducted me, and with your glory, you have taken me up.

For what is there for me in heaven? And what do I wish for on earth before You?

My body has failed, and my heart: O God of my heart, and God my portion, into eternity.

For behold, those who put themselves far from You will perish. You have perished all those who fornicate away from You.

But it is good for me to adhere to God, to put my hope in the Lord God, so that I may announce all Your prophecies, at the gates of the daughter of Zion.

Visualization

Did you have teachers in school, who told you to stop gawking out the window and quit daydreaming? I am those teacher's worst nightmare, because I am telling you to start daydreaming and don't stop. I want you to engage your imagination now like you did when you were a child. Nothing was impossible back then. Nothing was too outlandish to imagine. You had big dreams, but somewhere along the road you dropped those dreams because you began to believe it wasn't possible to attain them. It may be because your parents had other expectations for your career, or your friends laughed at you when you confided to them what you really wanted to do with your life. The great news is that it is never too late to regenerate those dreams. It's time today to pick up the pieces and refocus, rediscover, and receive your heart's desire. Remember, you can't lose anything in the universe.

Now that you've been developing your spiritual eyes, you're ready to practice visualization and receive results. Focus on and think about what you would like; pray about it, and see God answering you. Focus on the areas in your life that you want God to heal and recreate. Know that God still performs creation miracles and makeovers. Whether you need recreating in your career, family dynamics, your marriage, relationships with your co-workers, a friend, or your finances, God is ready to get started with your makeover. Don't doubt the effectiveness of visualization or your ability to attain success with this exercise. Believe you will receive what you are visualizing. God cannot be limited. His Love and generosity knows no boundaries. I tell my friends, 'When you believe, you will receive. When you doubt, you will strike out.' It's true.

I learned how to visualize at twenty-six. I wanted a suede coat. But not just any suede coat. I had specific details and I included them when I visualized my coat coming to me. Firstly, the color had to be burnt sienna. It had to be from Uruguay. Don't ask me why I chose Uruguay; there was no particular reason. The color and country came to me in a flash. I *saw* the label sewn to the coat's lining, *Made in Uruguay*. Of course it had to be the right size, a medium, or size seven. Last was the price. I was pushing the envelope of visualization on this point, but it didn't stop me. I wanted my perfect coat to be at the perfect price of $50, no more.

My conscious mind told me I was asking for the moon but, being a true believer in my ability to visualize, I stayed on course. I knew suede coats sold for much more than $50 but that didn't stop me from visualizing myself walking down the street in a burnt sienna suede coat, size seven, made in Uruguay and paying no more than $50 for it. I visualized the end result. This point is vital to achieving your goals when visualizing. When you can see the end result, and forget the middle part of *how* it will happen, your subconscious mind will lead you serendipitously. I paid no attention to visualizing a specific store; whether this perfect coat was in a mall, or on Main Street, I believed and accepted the thought it was coming to me. All I did was see myself wearing it. I did that twice. I released my wish and pictures to God and His universe and forgot about it.

Two months later, I happened to take a different route home from work (intuition led me). I spotted a store going out of business. I had exactly $50 in my wallet. I parked my Mustang, entered the shop and proceeded to the rear of the store where the coats were hung. Aha! There it was – a burnt sienna suede coat. Is this a coincidence? I thought. No, it can't be. This is my visualization unfolding naturally. I took the coat from its hanger to check the size. It was a size seven. I tried it on and it fit perfectly. I put the coat back on the hanger and knew it was time to turn over the price tag. The thought ran through my mind that there was no way this coat would cost $50. I reluctantly turned the tag, half expecting disappointment, but it read $49 No Tax. This was my first successful experience with visualizing but it wasn't to be my last.

Four months later, Penn State was playing Alabama in the Sugar Bowl. It was December 29th. My boss let the staff go home early for the holiday. For the past few days I had been wishing I was on my way to New Orleans to see the game, but I had no ticket, no hotel reservation, no plans and little money to get there. A trip like this should be planned and paid for months in advance. I left the office and headed home. After lunch I decided to meditate and visualize. Thoughts of my suede coat came to mind. If I had visualized only twice in the summer and received my suede coat in September, why shouldn't I be able to repeat a successful visualization and somehow get to New Orleans for the football game on Sunday, January 1st? If I did it once, I can do it again.

It was Friday afternoon, December 30th, at 2 pm when I began to visualize myself walking down Bourbon Street. I visualized and lost focus. I cleared my mind and began again. I *saw* myself walking down Bourbon Street and cheering at The Super Dome. The entire exercise lasted perhaps four minutes. At 2:20 pm an old friend, Bobby G., burst through the front door asking, 'Betsy! Do you want to go to New Orleans? I have five tickets for the Penn State game on Sunday.' Before I fainted from the shock, I answered yes to Bobby's question. It was tons of fun and loads of laughs all the way to New Orleans and back home to Pennsylvania.

When the Toronto Skydome opened in June of 1989, I made my way to one of the home games. Sitting close to third base, I looked up and across the field to the hotel windows and wished that someday I might watch a game from the Skydome Hotel. I had no idea how on earth that was ever going to happen on my salary, but I mentally told God which room it should be. It did not have to be the center room of the hotel, the room to the left of center would be fine. I visualized watching a game from that room for about thirty seconds and forgot about it.

A few months later, I happened to have lunch at The Hard Rock Café, inside Skydome. A gentleman sat beside me and asked what I did for a living. I told him I worked as a medical secretary, but I was there that day to cover the game for my girlfriend, who was the owner and editor of a Toronto community newspaper. I was the paper's only sports columnist. Immediately, I was invited upstairs to a room in the Skydome Hotel to meet this man's boss, an Irish publisher who owned a sports paper in Dublin. It just happened to be the room I had advised God I would like to watch a game from some day. My some day had arrived. I spent it chatting with the publisher's grandmother, while watching the game and making new friends from the Emerald Isle.

I have learned the lesson that nothing is impossible when your intention is clear and you cast out all doubt. Don't entertain doubt for a second. Believe in your ability to visualize accurately with positive results. Like me, if you lose your focus, just begin again and don't quit. Stick with it. These are just three examples of my wonderful results using visualization. My coat cost $49, the trip to New Orleans set me back about $150 and the baseball game was absolutely free. What would you like to co-create with God? He's ready to partner with you and respond to your requests. God isn't limited and neither are you.

The key to successful visualization is getting right to the end result. See yourself having whatever it is that you want. Forget the middle part. Forget *how* you are going to get to the successful conclusion. Just believe unwaveringly that you will. I have explained visualization to at least twenty-five friends over the years. Each one of them has wanted something specific to happen for them. Their hardest part is letting go of the how it will happen of visualization. Instead of eagerly getting started, they proceeded to ask me with high anxiety in their voice, 'How is this going to happen?' Like meditation, you must practice visualization and kept at it.

Don't become discouraged or begin to doubt. I only visualized wearing my suede coat twice before I found it. When a friend, who wanted to learn visualization heard this, she replied, 'Well, I am only going to do this exercise two times,' assuming she would only need two sessions to shift her personal relationship with her boyfriend to the next level. She had never meditated or visualized in all of her forty-five years. I knew she was going to need more time, just by her arrogant attitude and need to control him.

Like meditation, you must keep at it, not get discouraged and keep persevering. Keep your intentions pure and on a higher vibration. Don't ever attempt to control anyone because you will never succeed. That is Natural Law.

Begin visualization by going into the meditative state. Clear your mind of all thoughts. Empty your mind like you empty your waste basket. Let go of all negativity. See in your mind exactly what you want to come into your life. Don't be vague; be specific. This is vital to your visualization. The more specific you are the better results you'll achieve. Don't just think I want a job. That may bring a job with part-time hours and the minimum wage. Ask for more. Ask for exactly what you want. Shoot for the stars. If you wish to be the manager in your department, visualize meeting with your supervisor and accepting the promotion. See yourself moving into the manager's office and making it your own with your own style of décor. Imagine you need to have new business cards made with your new title embossed on them. Imagine, imagine, imagine. Ask God from your heart to grant and guide you to your heart's desire. He'll make sure you get it when your intention is pure.

If you are having a difficult time with a co-worker, see the two of you enjoying lunch together. That idea might not make sense to you due to past disagreements between the two of you. Imagine God in the middle of the situation with the two of you. He can restore and renew your relationship. Let go of the disagreements and see the relationship in a new light, His Light. Surround the two of you in God's White Light. Daily or nightly visualizations will speed up the manifestations of your desired results. Whether you visualize for more harmonious relationships, a better career, financial headway, or a better marriage, the sky isn't the limit. Devote ten minutes daily/nightly to your visualizations and soon you'll see your results materialize.

Can you visualize for a friend? Yes, you most certainly can. You can visualize and pray for any situation to improve. Ten years ago, my friend, Cassie, called me from California. Her mother-in-law had come to visit and decided to stay. My friend was distraught and at the end of her rope. I thought my friend meant her mother-in-law decided to stay an extra week. No, she had stayed an extra three months. I advised my girlfriend that I would pray her mother-in-law out of her home in California and back to her own home in Indiana. I was also going to visualize for the highest and the best coming to all involved parties. I could sense by the doubt in my friend's voice that she did not believe I could do this. I assured her I could.

Ten days later, I received a call from Cassie. Uh oh, I thought, here comes more complaining. Instead, I was happy to hear that Cassie was just back from the airport, after dropping her mother-in-law off at LAX to take her flight back home to Indiana. She had called to thank me for the visualizations and prayers. They had worked. I had no doubts; I just did not know the amount of time that would be necessary to achieve the desired result. It's vital whenever you visualize and pray for someone that you see the situation coming to a happy ending as this one did. Whether the situation is health, love or financial, see God working with you. He will bring it to pass.

The Circle of God's Love Meditation

I learned this meditation three decades ago, and I have used it successfully numerous times. I hope that you will too. Don't forget to say your thanks when finished. Begin your meditation by surrounding yourself in the White Light of God's Love. Imagine this Light emanating from the crown of your head, surrounding you down to the bottoms of your feet. Imagine a thick cord of this White Light rising from your solar plexus skyward, into the Hands of God the Creator. Then envision another cord of White Light flowing forth from your third eye, reaching out to what it is you are wishing and praying for. Contemplate this spiritual connection between you, the Creator, and your answered prayer. You may have a job interview coming up. In your meditation, envision God holding the cord of Light in His hand, and you throwing out the line of Light from your third eye to your new job. You may picture the building where the company is located, or envision interviewing with the manager, or see yourself at work already in your office. Yes, see yourself as having this job before you have even gone for your interview. Claim it in His Name. Thank Him and expect the best. When you live in grateful anticipation, believing and feeling like a deserving child of God, you'll receive your answer. God doesn't have any orphans. He gives us all a great inheritance.

Perhaps you're hoping to move to another city or to a different neighborhood in the city where you live. You would link with God with the White Light, and imagine the White Light flowing from your third eye to your desired location. You may see the type of house you would like. Be specific. If you like brick houses, see yourself connecting to the perfect brick bungalow or townhouse of your choice. Know that you deserve this house.

Feel deserving of receiving it. Realize that the house needs your loving touch as much as you desire to live in it and make it your own. There is no limitation to what you can envision and connect with and attract into your life. When you receive what you have been visualizing, remember to say thank You to God.

Chapter 10

Words are Powerful Thoughts are Things

On March 19, 2001, I was having my morning coffee at home. It was my birthday. I had the day to myself. I turned on a morning news show to see what developments had occurred in the world over night. My right eye felt irritated. I brushed my bangs away from my eyes but that didn't take away the odd sensation in my right eye. I noticed my vision dimming and the television screen shrinking. Something was happening to my 20/20 vision and I was beginning to feel scared. In less than five minutes, the vision in my right eye was completely gone. From all of the spiritual books I've read, and being a believing Christian, I did not panic, but remained calm. I was scared but calm. What was happening? I grabbed my health card, keys, my bus pass and said out loud, 'Francis, come with me. I'm all alone.'

I proceeded to the clinic at the top of my street. Once inside the examining room, I explained my frightening experience to the doctor. He decided he was going to give me an eye exam. I told him to save his time. I had perfect vision in my left eye but my right eye was a total write-off. He explained that in order to send me to the hospital, he had to administer the eye exam.

He stood on the spot where I would be reading the eye chart. He glanced at my file and said, 'Frances, stand over here.' Did I just hear the name he called me correctly? It wasn't my correct name but I took it as a fantastic omen that everything was going to be alright no matter how scary things got.

I knew who made him say that name and was so glad he did. It was a sign; as in visualization you accept the end result while not being concerned of the *how* of it. I accepted my complete healing at that moment and knew God had His hand on me. I knew I wasn't alone as I had told Francis thirty minutes earlier. I knew I would see again. When the doctor realized his error, he began to apologize profusely. An apology wasn't necessary. I was so happy to hear the name Frances. To me, this was confirmation that not only did Francis hear me at home, but he and God had given me a sign only we would understand. The gratitude I felt was immeasurable. Is it any wonder I love this angel so much. He's the best.

That day, I spent nine hours in the emergency room. I sat on a small stool outside an examination room for five hours before the neurosurgeon had time to see me. I often reflect on how I did not have a nervous breakdown sitting there alone with no family or friends with me for support, but a cloud of calm surrounded me. I knew it was my Francis who had wrapped his wings around me and kept me company and calm. A sense of heavenly serenity surrounded me all day and night at the hospital. I wasn't upset, I wasn't worried.

I finally saw the neurologist at 6 pm for five minutes and then he disappeared for another hour. I knew he was busy; the ER was filled with patients and under-staffed. I saw an eye surgeon, who tested my eyes again at 7 pm. She booked a CT scan for me for the next morning. After being tested, prodded, poked, asked if I had gone on a drinking or cocaine binge, she admitted she had no clue as to what had caused my blindness. I returned to see the neurologist downstairs in the ER. His best guess was that an airborne virus had settled in my right eye. He said he would see me tomorrow and sent me home.

The next day I had the CT scan and met seven more doctors. The neurologist advised me that he could have the visiting nurse come to my house three times a week and administer steroid shots. I asked him if there were any side effects that accompanied this treatment. There was just one; one in every ten thousand patients died instantly. I declined his kind offer and let the doctor know that I was living in an old Baptist church. Since he and the other doctors had no remedy for my predicament, I advised him that I was going home and I would let Dr. Jesus take charge of my case. That night, Francis had a special message for me. He told me my eyesight would return in nine weeks. Francis told me more in one sentence than nine doctors had in forty eight hours.

During this time of temporary blindness I fielded lots of questions from friends and acquaintances. Are you mad at God? Why aren't you blind in both eyes? Why would I ever entertain this idea? In some voices I heard a hint of ill will, as if they wished me total blindness instead of complete healing. I was careful to avoid those people; in fact, I went out of my way to avoid them. My answer to the first question was; no, I wasn't mad at God; I trusted Him completely. He wasn't punishing me. Perhaps He was purifying me. Maybe He wanted me to experience what it is like to be considered less that 100% healthy.

This blindness would give me a better understanding of how people with disabilities are treated in our society. I knew I was a compassionate person but I was becoming more compassionate. It made me appreciate simple things I had taken for granted before, like being able to put a key in a keyhole. I couldn't do that very well or find the handle on my coffee mug. What I wouldn't give to have my sense of depth perception back to normal.

Whatever God's reasons were, this situation was giving me a new perspective on illness and a new respect for the disabled. It was at this time that I happened to accidentally turn on a radio show and heard an author say, 'Illness is a friend, who has come to tell you the truth.' It was no coincidence that I turned on the radio at an unusual time and *accidentally* heard this author and healer. I was learning a lot. God had never put me through any trial that He couldn't get me through with His help and with Francis beside me.

I expected a complete healing, nothing less. I asked everyone, friends and foes alike, to see me healed. If they were going to speak about me, please don't say, 'Poor Betsy, she's going blind.' Instead, I requested them to state positively and confidently, 'It's great, Betsy is going to see again.' Some people got it, some didn't. Those that didn't were unable to lift their thinking out of the earth's vibration. They couldn't possibly see how this situation would ever improve. They couldn't grasp the concept of visualizing the best for me. They definitely didn't believe Francis existed let alone talked to me and was a healing angel.

Let this be a lesson for you. If ever you find yourself in similar circumstances, be sure to surround yourself with friends and relatives who never accept a negative word or thought. Surround yourself with people and the God Who loves you. Tune into your healing angels.

I cranked my prayer time up a notch or two on my days off. One Sunday, I began to pray the psalms, read scripture, recite the rosary, and play Mahaliah Jackson gospel CDs for ten straight hours. I'm sure my neighbors thought I was holding my own revival. I was consistent with keeping a set prayer time each weekday. My prayer practice strengthened me and gave me renewed hope. I praised God, out loud, thanking Him for all past favors, and reminded Him how I expected my complete healing from Him. He created this world with His word. As one of His children I believed I had the same ability to speak words and recreate my health with Him. I kept praying and praising Him out loud. I thanked Him in advance for my complete recovery. God can't resist answering you when you thank Him in advance.

I decided to sleep with the Bible beside me at eye level every night. There is God's Power in that book. I wanted it to hit me right in the eye. I received a get well card from someone who had stolen from me ten years earlier. I sat down and forgave her and everyone who had ever hurt me. This was the turning point in my healing. From that day forward, my eyesight began to return. There is power in forgiving. At the end of nine weeks my eyesight was fully restored just as my angel, Francis, had promised.

Words are Real

Just today, May 13, 2010, I received an email from someone who wrote, 'Not knowing this is killing me.' I hope not knowing your future moment to moment doesn't hurt you, or this woman. It certainly won't kill me, but apparently, today's emailer is on the road to making herself sick with her thoughts, words and way of thinking. I promptly replied, admonishing her to edit her thoughts and words.

What you think and say holds power and energy. Your words will manifest in your life. So will your thoughts. You don't need to visualize them. They will show up automatically. So be aware of your words. What you say out loud will go forth into the universe and bring you exactly what you say, sing or chant out loud. Here are just a few of the expressions I hear every day: 'I'm sick of my job.' This person is under a doctor's care for ulcers. 'My boyfriend and I do not see eye to eye.' This person is having an eye exam in three weeks for blurred vision. Is there any wonder why? 'I work with a bunch of back stabbers.' This woman was asking me for medical advice about pain radiating from the middle of her back. I am not a doctor but I recommended she visit a chiropractor to adjust her spine while she adjusts her attitude.

Please remember, your words can make you sick. Or, they can heal you. The choice is yours. Use your words wisely. Think before you speak and you'll be much healthier and happier. Also, for all of you deeply in love who exude enthusiastically, 'I love him/her to death' please change this loving statement to: 'I love him/her to life.'

Watch What You Say

Now, it's my turn to admit my own guilt. I should take my own advice. Sometimes I do. Other times I don't and I pay for it dearly. You think I would know by now to heed my own words. In April of 2008, after a severe winter in Toronto, I told a friend, 'I am not sitting in front of my computer this summer. I am going to get out more. I need to walk, get more exercise, see more of my neighbors and read more books. I need to get to the library. I need to disconnect from this computer. This winter was brutal. I need to get out into the sunshine.' The very next day my computer crashed. It was as if it had heard me and granted me my wish. What I said came true in less than twenty-four hours, and I did end up at the library using their free computer until mine was restored. How is that for the universe taking me at my word?

Faced with having to buy a new computer or have mine repaired, I decided Positive Affirmations were the route to take. I sat down and wrote, 'God gives me a free computer.' I wrote that several times and thought, nay, I am limiting my God. I started a new affirmation: God gives me three computers. I wrote it over and over. I left out the word free and new, because I trusted God to supply my need, free or not, refurbished or new, it didn't matter, I expected Him to come through. Within a week, I had three free computers.

Instead of reacting on a human level, cursing, swearing, fussing and expecting the worst to continue, my attitude took a spiritual turn for the better. Jesus said, 'Ask and you shall receive.' I put it out there and expected my good to arrive. I took Him at His Word and He delivered. So when you are facing challenges in life, watch how you react. Watch and keep your emotions in check. Watch what you say. What Job feared came upon him (Job 1:2-3). You don't want to end up like that. You want to experience Divine Providence, Jehovah Jireh: God will provide. He provided for me and He's ready and able to provide for you. Whether it is a financial need, an emotional one or an illness that needs to be healed, God is ever at the ready to touch you and be in touch with you.

Banish Negative Emotions

I've met many angry people through the years. I advised all of them to let go of the idea of revenge. Nothing will boomerang faster in your life than when you want revenge. If you feel wronged by your employer, a friend, your mate, a relative, whatever you do, don't curse them, because every evil thing you wish upon them will return to you faster and worse than what you wished upon them. This is Universal Law. Don't direct your energy plotting revenge. Give it over to God. He knows what is in your heart, so keep your thoughts and emotions pure and positive.

Whenever someone hurts you, slights you, does you wrong, pray for the highest and the best for them and yourself. This will make all the difference in the outcome of your situation. When you let go and let God take care of it for you, you will see wonderful positive results. A neighbor of mine was angry and filled with hatred toward a co-worker. Her co-worker had received the promotion my neighbor had been hoping for. She gave me reason after reason why she should have been promoted instead of her rival. After calming my friend, I asked her to pray with me. Together, we handed this work situation over to Father God. I asked that the right promotion come into my friend's life, one that would be better than this opportunity that she felt she had missed. We blessed her co-worker and asked for her to be prospered. We then gave thanks in advance to God, for sending my friend another opportunity to replace the one she felt she had lost. We ended our prayer session and I advised my friend to hold the thought and feeling of expecting the best.

Although you may be feeling disappointment today, visualize yourself where you would be your happiest. Imagine having your dream job come to you. When you expect the best and you send out that vibration, the best will come into your life. This too is Universal Law. Within two weeks, I received a call from my friend. She was no longer holding onto resentment. She sounded happy and upbeat. She had just received a telephone call from an employer she had interviewed with six months earlier. She had not gotten that job, but as fate would have it, the person who was initially selected was moving to another country because of her husband's job. Instead of cursing, instead of wishing ill on another, instead of hanging onto her negative emotions, my friend had been offered her dream job by changing her attitude and behavior. Praying, keeping her thoughts and words positive and thanking God in advance brought it to pass.

It's vital when you are presented with a challenging situation in your life to stay positive. Even when the situation is bleak, don't envision the worst; see the best coming to you and it will arrive at the appointed time. Don't dwell on the worst outcome possible. Visualize the best outcome for everyone involved. Banish any negative thoughts and the negative emotions attached to them. Give your undivided attention to God and let Him provide the answer. Depend on Him to resolve your problems. Your problems, situations, unpleasant scenarios, will be transformed when you put them in His hands. Place yourself there too. When you are at a dead end and can't come up with an answer, turn to the One, Who knows what you need, before you ask. Whenever I come in contact with negative people who overreact and effuse negativity, I use the following prayer:

I am a spirit. I am a spiritual being. I am on earth experiencing this negative behavior which has no place in my life or home. I realize this person is at a lower level of their Spiritual Development. Therefore, I bless them and ask the angels to neutralize this situation. Please transform this situation with the grace of God. Let them receive their right solution. Thank You, God and angels.

Expect the Best

One day while visiting a friend, I noticed she had a plethora of cold tablets, nasal sprays, back rub ointments and decongestants sitting on her kitchen table. I asked what she was doing with all these cold and flu remedies in the middle of August. Her reply surprised me, 'Oh, I'm stocking up for when I get sick this winter.' My friend expected to get sick just as she had last year and the year before that. She was scheduling illness into her life. I explained to her that every time she would see these products in her medicine cabinet, she was impressing on her subconscious mind to prepare for illness that was headed her way. She was ready to be sick. I suggested she put them away and impress her subconscious mind with the idea of perfect health. She should visualize herself enjoying the winter in good health, not sniffling her way through it. She reluctantly listened, packed the flu remedies up and placed them in the back of her clothes closet. She became interested in natural remedies during the fall and learned the benefits of cayenne pepper. When she felt a cold coming on in December, she drank a glass of ice water with a pinch of cayenne pepper in it and her cold symptoms disappeared in ninety minutes.

Just yesterday, someone came to visit and asked me what I saw with her health. I told her I saw blue/green in her aura, which represents good health. Her next sentence was, 'So, what should I be worried about?' I was disappointed in her response. I thought she was a bit more enlightened than to embrace the idea of worry. I am saddened that so many people are expecting to hear bad news and can't wait to start worrying. They don't want to waste a minute being happy and grateful, when they can focus on the worst happening and begin to worry in advance. That's a total waste of energy. Use your energy wisely, by not worrying needlessly.

More Exercises

Here are several exercises for you to use to continue your development.

Have you ever thought of all the energy that is not used in the world? There is a lot of energy going to waste. The next time you're walking down the street, say to yourself, 'I take in all the energy not being used.' Repeat this statement and imagine the energy flowing into your soul. Imagine your body and soul being infused with white energy. If you are a sports fan and enjoy attending events, it's a prime time to absorb the surge of energy when your team scores a goal, touchdown, or homerun. Whether you are a football, baseball, hockey, soccer, lacrosse, or rugby fan, when the fans go wild cheering, make a conscious effort to absorb the energy they are sending around the arena. I even take the energy when the other team scores. Energy is energy.

When you are trying to find an answer to a problem, especially if it is work or looking for a new house/apt., take a walk in the area where you would like to work/reside. As you walk, you'll be using energy and visualization together to attain your goal. Imagine the White Light, emanating from your crown chakra, connecting you to your proper place of employment, or your perfect home. See yourself attaining the perfect job or perfect residence. I have shared this exercise with friends who found exactly what they were wishing for, whether employment or a new residence. It even worked for a friend looking for the perfect pooch. She kept the picture of her new bulldog in her mind as she strolled home from work every afternoon and threw out her energy. Five days later, she answered an ad in the daily newspaper placed by a breeder of English Bulldogs. It was no surprise to her that the woman with the puppies for sale lived within two blocks of her office building. She had walked by the breeder's condo, emanating energy every evening, while visualizing walking her perfect puppy. Now she walks her dog every day just as she had pictured it.

The following two exercises are for anyone needing an energy boost. If you don't have a tree in your yard, visit a nearby park. Sit up against a tree with your spine touching the tree trunk. Sit quietly and ask the tree to send you energy. This exercise can be done for five minutes, or however long you wish to commune with the tree. Of course, when you leave, don't forget to thank the tree. If sitting on the ground isn't for you, find a tree, perhaps an old oak tree, with large roots rising out of the ground. Place one foot on the root and ask the tree to send you energy from Mother Earth. Thank the tree and continue on with your day. I often do this at an intersection close by my home. It looks like I am taking a rest, until the traffic light turns green. Only the tree and I know what I'm really doing.

Say What You Want
Say out loud what you want. Talk to yourself and tell yourself the wonderful things God is going to do for you today. Declare it, decree it, and claim it, in His Name. Maybe you want to bring in the correct life partner. In that case, chant love for eleven minutes a day. When I chant, I focus not just on the word and what it represents to me, but also on my throat chakra. I visualize the energy radiating out into the world from my throat, connecting me to what I am claiming.

Years ago, in development class, another clairvoyant recommended placing a rubber band around our wrists and snapping it any time we students were tempted to utter a negative statement. Not being a masochist, I opted for studying the Book of Proverbs and committed some of the following to memory. I hope they help you to watch your thoughts, words and intentions, as they instilled in me the importance of only pronouncing positive words with the best of intentions.

Proverbs to Guard Your Words

13:3 Whoever guards his mouth guards his soul. But whoever gives no consideration to his speech shall experience misfortunes.

15:2 The tongue of the wise adorns knowledge.

15:4 A peaceful tongue is a tree of life.

16:24 Careful words are a honeycomb: Sweet to the soul and healthful to the bones.

17:13 Whoever repays evil for good, evil shall not withdraw from his house

18:21 Death and life are in the power of the tongue

26:22 The words of a whisperer seem simple, but they penetrate to the innermost parts of the self.

Affirmations

Love

My right life partner enters my life now, effortlessly and through Divine Guidance.

My angels connect me now with my right life partner under God's Grace.

Divine Guidance leads me to my right partner. We recognize each other on the soul level.

I bless _____ out of my life. He/she will soon meet his/her right partner in God's time and by His Grace.

My partner and I resolve our differences and issues by Divine Guidance. We trust God to guide our paths.

I send love out into God's universe and love returns to me.

Love is my Divine Right. I deserve to be loved unconditionally today and always.

I have a life filled with meaning, purpose and love. I am

blessed and grateful.

Love is a gift to me from God. I value love and share it with everyone I meet.

I give love generously to all. The more love I give the more love multiplies in my life.

Love soothes, love calms, love guides, love heals. Love dissolves fear. I am safe.

Money

My cup of plenty overflows through Divine Guidance and Providence.

I am led to green pastures of plenty through the Grace of God.

God is my Supplier. His gifts have no limit.

God delights in my prosperity. I embrace His good gifts.

When I share I have more to spare. I delight in helping others.

My God is the best Banker. He guides my Financial Footsteps. He guides my Financial Decisions.

I bless my bills and pay them happily.

As I tithe the tide of prosperity rushes in to meet my needs and blesses me.

Receiving a small portion predicts my prosperity. Divine overflow is on its way to me. I see it soon.

Money manifests in my life through God's mysterious ways.

Career

I work from my heart chakra.

My career helps me fulfill my Divine destiny.

God connects me to my right career. He is guiding my career choices today.

My right career blesses me and all who work with me.

My career is chosen from a spiritual place.

When I choose from a point of love my right money comes with my Divine right choice.

My Divine right career is my dharma.

My Divine right career comes to me in ways I cannot imagine. Now is the Divine right time.

There is no doubt with my career choice. All is crystal clear to me now.

I move towards my Divine right career as it moves closer to me.

Divine doors open and give me my Divine right employment.

Health

This illness is in my life to teach me Divine Truth.

I am not afraid. God leads me to my cure now.

God now directs me to my right doctors and healers. I listen to His leads.

My cure arrives by God's Divine Grace.

When I am healed I will help others to heal.

This illness is a teacher. I am a student learning God's Laws of Healing.

There are no incurable illnesses only attitudes that need spiritual adjustment.

I manifest the faith of the woman who touched the hem of Christ's Robe. Her faith healed her. My faith heals me now.

God and my angels heal me as I sleep.

Healing can come in stages. God is with me at every stage.

God is healing me now. Thank You, God.

In Closing

I hope that this book has guided you to a closer connection with God, your Creator and the Source of all good in your life. May you sense His touch in your life. God bless you today and always.

BOOKS

O is a symbol of the world, of oneness and unity. In different cultures it also means the "eye," symbolizing knowledge and insight. We aim to publish books that are accessible, constructive and that challenge accepted opinion, both that of academia and the "moral majority."

Our books are available in all good English language bookstores worldwide. If you don't see the book on the shelves ask the bookstore to order it for you, quoting the ISBN number and title. Alternatively you can order online (all major online retail sites carry our titles) or contact the distributor in the relevant country, listed on the copyright page.

See our website www.o-books.net for a full list of over 500 titles, growing by 100 a year.

And tune in to myspiritradio.com for our book review radio show, hosted by June-Elleni Laine, where you can listen to the authors discussing their books.

MySpiritRadio